The Game Changer

To My Friend Kiana, I Believe in You! You Changed Your Game! keep! Going. Love! Jamie

Inspirational Stories that Changed Lives

Compiled by Iman Aghay

Spotlight PUBLISHING
Goodyear, AZ

The Game Changer (Volume 4): Inspirational Stories That Changed
Lives

ISBN: 978-1-7341855-1-5

Ordering Information:

Copies of this book may be ordered directly from
www.mylifechangingmoment.com

Website: **www.mychangingmoment.com**

Cover Illustration Adobe Prints
Cover Design Angie Anayla

Published by Spotlight Publishing, Goodyear AZ

TABLE OF CONTENTS

INTRODUCTION

I've been working with entrepreneurs and other successful professionals for the past sixteen years. As a business mentor, I see the complex interworking of an entrepreneur's life. I have the privilege of knowing what goes on behind the scenes. I am humbled when I see what it takes for entrepreneurs to realize their achievements.

The Game Changer Book Series is a collection of these behind-the-scene stories—stories that most people never realize have laid the foundation for a successful business or company. These stories are personal, connected to the authors' hearts, and many of them are being shared for the first time with you, our reader. As I read this collection, I could not stop thinking about this old adage: *"Everyone you meet is fighting a battle you know nothing about! Be kind, always…."*

This book reveals some of the hardest times and darkest moments that entrepreneurs live through. Their experiences are real and deeply personal. Many of the chapters tell of bad choices and overcoming mistakes. However, all of them share something in common: a turning point—the turning point that changed the author's life forever. These stories are very dear to each author, and I am honored to be able to share their experiences with you. I hope that each of these stories touches you as deeply as I have been touched.

Iman Aghay

Introduction

Entrepreneur Connection

By Kimberly Hobscheid

I love being an entrepreneur.

The freedom to focus on your own purpose. To pursue your passion. To create new possibilities in the world. But I wasn't always an entrepreneur. Just a few years ago, things were very different. I remember the evening when I realized I needed a change.

It was eleven o'clock at night. I was in my office at work, looking over the latest initiative Corporate was asking me to roll out to my team.

And, I was miserable.

Not because of the late hours; I didn't mind the schedule. Over the past decade and a half, I had worked my way up the corporate ladder to a director-level position, where I was now responsible for a large region with hundreds of people and five states. Along the way, I had built a team full of inspired and joyful people who understood where we were going, and who felt supported in getting there. We had fun together, leaning on our different strengths and as a result, we performed well as a team. We were a tight community.

And yet, I was unhappy. So how did I get here?

During my tenure, I had been a part of all kinds of wonderful initiatives and new ideas at Corporate. I had started at the bottom, learned the ropes before climbing the ladder rapidly. I began to mentor others. When someone couldn't understand the 'why', I enjoyed shedding light on the backstory and helping them get it. And when they understood, I felt like I had won too. We were surpassing all of our budget goals and having fun doing it.

As we grew, other offices and regions asked for the same training our team was getting. I didn't have anything formal written up but their request inspired me. I put together a collaborative team which included five members representing each of our regions came together with ease, and we assembled a systematic process that explained both what to do and why. When enthusiastic reviews and success stories came back from the field, I felt like I had won again. We had created something powerful for the good of the company. By sharing what worked well for each of us, we helped the entire community, causing a powerful ripple effect.

My heart sang. I was full of pride at what we had accomplished.

But, in the last two years of my tenure there, things started to really change. Our headquarters' executive team recently experienced several resignations, many of which came as a shock. A few of the promotions that took place afterward were done under unclear circumstances and without explanation. The tone of the company was changing. There was infighting at the highest levels as the new executive team worked to prove themselves. Several initiatives came out with conflicting messaging and didn't seem to fit the business or culture. And, uncharacteristically, they weren't asking any of us for input.

I went to the company headquarters to see what was going on. In the past, I had enjoyed visiting Corporate. Every time I walked the halls, I would visit each of the different departments — Legal, Accounting, Finance, Human Resources, Operations, and Marketing. These groups were full of intelligent and creative people who were experts in their fields. They were integral to my region's success and the impact we had on the world. I was very grateful to them. Many of these amazing people were my friends as well as colleagues.

But this time things felt tense everywhere I went. When my boss greeted me, I instantly noticed he had aged quite a bit since the last time I saw him. Though he was smiling from ear-to-ear, it didn't quite reach his eyes. He listened to my concerns but dismissed them just as quickly, telling me that my team and I were going to be just fine as long as we were implementing the new changes without making any waves. He explained the culture was changing as it was due to challenges in other territories. And that there was no need for our suggestions or input because only compliance would be valued.

The Game Changer

My heart sank on the drive home. The impact on company decisions, and the influence I thought I had, was gone. It occurred to me that in this new culture the higher-ups were solely interested in people following directions - without contributing their ideas or opinions. And definitely without any need for their passion or heart. Even though I had spent a decade and a half at this organization, in this new culture - I had become replaceable. If these new initiatives coming out included things that I personally didn't agree with, I could implement them, or I could leave.

Have you ever found yourself going down the corporate road, and then discovering that the company values no longer match your own? That they were going in one direction and you wanted to go in the other. I was feeling crosswise with my own principles. Promoting someone else's dream. In doing so, I had fallen out of integrity with myself.

I thought about the people I had brought on board. The community I had built; the community that trusted me. I had a crisis of faith believing now that if this company I had helped build could turn so quickly, then any company could.

Within a month, I decided to leave corporate and go full-time into entrepreneurship. I believed that, as an entrepreneur, I could control this problem because I would be the captain of my own ship. And, as long as I was on my own, I would never have to betray myself, my values, my people, or my community ever again.

Luckily, I had an advantage. I had created a couple of side-hustles before and was familiar with the life cycle of small businesses. I knew it was not as easy as everyone thinks it would be. I knew of people who left their corporate with the idea that going out on their own will be natural. But what they've taken for granted is the system that enabled them to be who they were in the corporate world in the first place. An organization has many layers of support built into itself. The community. The team. The mentors. People who strengthen your confidence when things felt confused or unsteady. People who would celebrate wins with you.

But when you start out on your own, that is literally what we are: alone. Yes, this has its advantages, but it has its drawbacks as well.

I was on my own.

Kimberly Hobscheid

No team.
No support.
No community.

I was lonely.

As humans, we fundamentally need community. We need it for two reasons — when you have challenges, you receive support; when you have wins, you get to share those wins with others.

Now that I was living life as a full-time entrepreneur, I had no one to share it with. I felt incomplete. When I got stuck, I eventually figured things out on my own, but it took a lot more time and energy. When I had a win, I was alone in my success and that left me feeling empty. The business was a modest success and I was surviving, but I wasn't having any fun. I wasn't thriving. My business went flat. My excitement waned and I lost interest in seeing it grow. I was feeling the drain of being an entrepreneur.

Then one day, I was procrastinating on the needs of my fledgling business and an idea struck me. And it had to do with avocado trees.

At my house, there are five avocado trees clustered together in one area of our yard. They are tall, strong plants with wide green leaves. Avocado trees, biologically, are very unique in the plant world. Biologists describe them as "uniquely perfect" in that they have both the pistol and stamen -the male and female parts in the same flower. Scientifically speaking, they should be able to stand alone and cross-pollinate within themselves.

But while they have the equipment to do this, evolution has come up with an unexpected twist in the tree flower itself. The flower of the tree it only blossoms for two days. The first day, the female part of the flower opens for a brief window of time, between two to four hours. During this time, it can receive pollen. However, the male parts are not yet exposed. On the second day, the male parts of the flower open to release their pollen.

You see, technically, while the avocado trees have everything they need to live in isolation, they have developed in a way that makes it nearly impossible for a tree to cross-pollinate itself and thrive. They need to rely on the blossoming flowers from other trees nearby. In essence, they need community.

And there was my pivot point.

Of course! Just like the avocado trees, as entrepreneurs, we may be fully capable of doing things independently as we have all the proper pieces and parts. But the truth is… we need each other.

We need diverse opinions. Clever ideas. The wealth of knowledge that is contained within the many. We need theories and understanding of others in order to become our best selves. We need support and collaboration. We need to have that cross-pollination to actually thrive. We need community.

That's why I created Entrepreneurs Rocket Fuel.

I wanted to construct a network of entrepreneurs who would support each other, share experiences, and to feel part of a team. To bring together people who want to give back and are willing to support each other with what they have learned. A community to go to when they are struggling and need help.

I am filled with hope as this community grows and blossoms. It is offering me the opportunity to both contribute and receive. Our community members have shared massive amounts of practical and insightful information. Inspiration. Answers. We are creating a trusted community where there is support, give and take, and cross-pollination to help everybody thrive. And that is what I needed to put the happiness back in my day.

The truth is, not one of us knows it all. Getting help from others in a trusted community fulfills a human need for support. And conversely, sharing knowledge with people who require it meets the intrinsic need of our contribution to something greater than ourselves.

This is a place where entrepreneurs can be individuals yet at the same time, they can belong, connect, and grow.

Kimberly Hobscheid

I am hopeful this community is an inspiration to others where they can

achieve their genius, in whatever form it takes.

Welcome to the community.
Come, and thrive.

Kimberly Hobscheid

Kimberly Hobscheid is an award-winning international inspirational public speaker, best-selling author, audiobook producer, six-time entrepreneur.

She is the creator of **Entrepreneurs Rocket Fuel,** an active community of Entrepreneurs, looking to contribute, connect and grow with other entrepreneurs. Her vision is to inspire all entrepreneurs, to achieve their genius, in whatever way that is.

Kimberly, is the mother of two and an adventure seeker, who has hiked sections of the Pacific Crest Trail, navigated Class IV rapids with one of Costa Rica's female Olympic medal-winning whitewater champions, sailed down the coast of Mexico on a 42-foot Yankee Clipper, and traversed 200 miles on horseback through Canada's Jasper National Park. Her motto is "live life out loud"

Kimberly has been a guest speaker in cities worldwide, inspiring people to get to where they want to go. Her specialty is turning dreams into reality.

Connect with Kimberly:
LinkedIn: www.linkedin.com/in/kimberlyhobscheid
Web: www.entrepreneursrocketfuel.com
Facebook:
https://www.facebook.com/groups/entrepreneursrocketfuel
Instagram: https://instagram.com/imhearingstories/
Twitter: www.twitter.com/HearingStories
Twitter: www.twitter.com/BigDataAnalyzed
Contact: Kimberly@entrepreneursrocketfuel.com

Kimberly Hobscheid

To view Kimberly's Game Changer Interview, scan the QR Code below or click on this link: https://youtu.be/MyaqQK1_GJk

-2-

Dreams Are Like Fluffy White Clouds

By Ali Lankerani

As a child, do you remember looking up at the blue sky and marveling at the fluffy white clouds? Did you ever think about the story of *Jack and the Beanstalk* and wonder what it would be like to live up there? I know I did.

For most of us, the wonder is gone by the time we grow up, or we experience disappointment as an airplane passes through the clouds with ease because you realize they are no different than the steam coming from your kettle. The clouds from our childhood never changed, but in the process of growing up, the magic was lost. As kids, we would whine the entire length of the car ride, but as parents, we were driven mad when we heard the kids complain until we reached our destination.

As a mentor of mine once said, in reality 'anticipation is greater than realization'.

Ever since I started working at 16, I was already thinking about my retirement so I could live out my dreams. And doing it all by 35, to be exact! I believed that if you were to live a productive and active life of 70 years (with anything after that as a bonus), then it would be fair to have to slave away the first half of your life. I was willing to trade my youth learning, improving, working, and saving in order to enjoy life and live it according to my priorities later on. I even had a reverse clock counting down to my retirement. As always, life doesn't happen on your timeline.

But by the time I was 40, I had moved into my beachfront dream home, was driving the car of my dreams and raising two wonderful kids. I had traveled and visited a dozen countries, I felt spiritually connected, had a great circle of friends, and had successfully supported my wife in launching her now thriving business. I had an abundance of free time to do with as I pleased. I clearly felt I was living the best years of my life — I wasn't too young as to be poor and inexperienced, but not too old as to be frail and out of touch with the modern world. I had just the right amount of health, experience, and means to enjoy what life had to offer. All I had to do was continue living that life for the rest of my days.

Only, I caught myself feeling increasingly frustrated and unhappy.

Once I got over the thrill of 'making it' and started living, the realities of life started to settle in. And in that moment, I realized I was no longer the same person. Every night I went to bed asking myself, *There has to be more to life than this. But what else is there?* There was always the possibility of experiencing new things, having more fun, spending more time with my family, and traveling, but in the end, it was just more of the same. I wondered, *Was this a case of 'anticipation being greater than realization'?*

I've heard of people coming out of retirement because they couldn't stand being idle, but I was quite happy with the retirement part. So that wasn't it. And, I believe if you're good at something, it doesn't always mean it's your calling. I wasn't going to fill my days doing things I was good at just to keep myself busy. I recalled my mentor's words from years before: 'Knowledge without implementation leads to frustration and depression'. This made me ask myself, *What knowledge was I not implementing that was leading to my frustration and depression?*

A memory came to me one day as I was staring at the ocean outside of my beachfront condo. It was a few years back in 2013 and I was at my aunt's house in Tehran, Iran. We were in the middle of the living room looking at centuries-old paintings of my ancestors from Paris and Germany. A proud fact about my family is that I come from a long line of old-world merchants. Over the years, I've heard stories of them finding love in India, escaping the Russian revolution, and experiencing entrepreneurial opportunities all over Europe. As we went through the art, my aunt pulled out a notebook that had my maternal family tree in it. I could trace my lineage to a contemporary poet, a rebel freedom fighter, a great-uncle who was caught in a plot to assassinate Hitler, industrialists who brought electricity to the north of Iran, an honorary citizen who received the key to the city of Hamburg, philanthropists who set up the first orphanage in the country — the list went on and on!

Then there was my absolute favorite. It was a magical story I had heard since childhood, linking me as the 42nd descendant of a Persian emperor.

Over the years, I had studied him extensively. He built one of the largest empires in human history and his reign was considered part of the golden era of the extensive Persian dynasty. During that time, it is said that nearly half of the earth's population was considered to be Persian. He was adamant about establishing and stabilizing trade routes along the northern sections of his empire, all the way from China to the Roman Empire, later known as the Silk Road. He ordered the knowledge from all corners of his vast empire to be gathered and compiled into one library. If this ancestor hadn't made the effort to do so, these ancient pearls of wisdom would have been lost forever as the burning of the Library of Alexandria had not happened long before. Scholars estimate this single event as one of the greatest tragedies in human history and set humanity's progress back by a thousand years.

About 200 years later, the contents of his library found its way across northern Africa and Europe, where it sparked the beginnings of the Renaissance and the Age of Enlightenment. Without it, Greek philosophy, the scientific method, the Industrial Revolution, and the modern world as we know it would not have been possible. The memory struck me, and I thought, *What a legacy! But what was to be* my *legacy?* In that moment, I knew what I was missing. What I had been searching for wasn't a thing, an experience, or a certain quality in life — it was my purpose.

As kids, we love to dream about what we will be when we grow up. But as we grow up, we become institutionalized through school and learn that our dreams and passions come second to that of society. We end up dulling our senses to cope with the authoritative reality and numbing ourselves to our passions. We climb corporate ladders with the intent to excel under society's ideals, yet many of us find ourselves succeeding at the top of ladders we never intended to climb. Trying to find your way back down the ladder in order to locate the correct one, then climbing once again is discouraged, painful, and at times, downright daunting. It takes time to connect with our childhood passions once more. And lastly, it takes courage to go after them.

I believe you have three choices in life:

> 1). Stay on top of the wrong ladder living out someone else's dream;

2). End it tragically by jumping off; or
3). Take your chances, climb down and go after your own passion and purpose.

I chose the third option.

It took me some time to dig deep and find those old passions again. After 23 years of schooling and a couple of decades of work, my dreams were certainly buried. But I was determined. I started with the earliest childhood memories and hobbies before working my way back to the present. This lead me to the legacy of philanthropic efforts to establish an orphanage in Iran, seeing TV images of state-owned children left in horrible conditions in Romania as the Soviet Union and European countries in the Eastern Bloc crumbled, and the AIDS epidemic in Africa affecting pregnant single moms and children.

Then there was my training as a physician, treating kids, educating parents, changing lives, and being a parent. Suddenly it all started to come together. The thing that had eluded me since my undergraduate days. The cure for my frustration and depression. The cause I would be happy to dedicate the rest of my life to. And one which utilized my knowledge and expertise.

I had found my ladder that would lead me to my legacy. I would be able to stand against injustice towards those who were unable to fend for themselves, the ones that would be shaping humanity's future. I created an online course called Nesting Amazing Kids, then set up the Amazing Parents Network under my organization, Optimal Beginnings (optimalbeginnings.info), where it will help parents to optimize their child's potential, giving them the best chance possible to become leaders, impacting the world in a positive way for generations to come.

With my new purpose, the successes of the past no longer became an end to themselves; they became the stepping-stones towards my goal. My failures served as learning opportunities and guiding posts. Now, daily routines that originally felt insignificant and any free time I had all went towards serving my new dream. Most importantly, my family is the foundation, along with my friends as the support, on which this legacy will be built.

If you're in search of 'making it', remember that 'anticipation is greater than realization'. Be careful what you ask for because if it's not for your true purpose, then it may be nothing more than fluffy white clouds.

To view Ali's Game Changer interview scan the QR Code below or click on this link: https://youtu.be/-Xt0d8sJAP8

Ali Lankerani

Ali Lankerani

Ali Lankerani, affectionately known by his patients as Dr. L, is a clinical neuroscientist with a background in chiropractic medicine. Dr. L currently runs an online course that supports new parents and their children and encourages healthy, growing relationships between them: Nesting Amazing Kids - How to Raise Happy and Healthy Kids and Enjoy the Process! Dr. L is internationally published, was twice-voted as one of America's Top Doctors, hosts the TV channel Optimal Beginnings has additional training in Traditional Chinese Medicine and Acupuncture and ran an award-winning private practice helping kids with Autism Spectrum Disorders. Dr. L's vision and mission for the future is threefold.

First, to devise a global non-profit network operating collaboratively with governments worldwide to ensure the safety, health, education, and productivity of new and expecting mothers and their children in order to thrive.

Second, to create a grassroots Brain-Based Healthcare movement so doctors and individuals approach health with a natural, top-down approach. At the core of his message, Dr. L believes helping people understand that working with their body instead of against it, individuals can bring about not only their own healthy lifestyle, but also can bring about not only their own healthy lifestyle, but also can positively impact the community, their environment, and their entire social structure.

And third, to build a Health & Potential Based Education program rooted in the natural development of children to foster their optimum potential - one which nurtures each child's God-given gifts, cherishes their zest for lifelong learning, and helps support them in their quest for personal fulfillment.

Dr. L stands strong for the acceptance and fulfillment of every human being's potential, and rallies against oppression, inequality, and ignorance. He is passionate about improving himself personally and takes to heart his part in making the world a better place for future generations. His ultimate desire and mission in life is to leave a legacy to further the fostering of our children's potential.

Dr. L enjoys mountaineering, European motorsports, and music and participates in Chinese martial arts with his children. Currently, he is gearing up to summit Mt. Aconcagua and hike the Himalayas. Ultimately, he wants to climb Mt. Vinson in Antarctica and ski sled to the South Pole. Dr. L enjoys being the active father of his two Amazing Kids and proudly serves as the founder of Amazing Parents' Network. You can find him regularly speaking at a variety of venues nationwide and internationally on subjects within his passions including health, lifestyle, and personal and child development.

Want to know more? We invite you to reach Dr. L at:

Website: www.Optimalbeginnings.info
Email: info@optimalbeginnings.info

Ali Lankerani

Out of the "Blackberry Bushes" and onto the "Cleared Path"

By Kathleen Kent

Today is a day of rest and time with my cat. I returned yesterday from an intensive 3-day event held in a Phoenix home with 40+ other people. We are all seeking to share our own unique message to make a positive impact on the world. I am emotionally charged, physically exhausted, psychologically centered, and spiritually floating in a state of wonder.

Although the 3-day event was on the topic I expected, the 5-day total experience has opened "doors" inside me that I had closed. I normally stay in a hotel by myself, but I chose to stay with 8 other people in a B&B home with a pool. I am so very grateful I made that choice. I had many one-on-one conversations with some inspiring people, my peers, and now my friends. I write this with a deeper understanding of myself. This 5-day experience provided a nurturing environment for me to evolve from a "lesser than" to an "equal to" state of being. I return to Seattle vastly different – I am a peer – not aspiring to be.

I am a lifelong learner.

Most of my learning has been from the school of "hard knocks."

I grew up in an alcoholic home… lots of dysfunction and many violent fights. At somewhere around 4-ish, I assumed the impossible role of trying to keep the peace and protect my younger brothers from my parents' rage. We had a rough home life. My grandparents ended up selling their orchard in Manson and moved to Chelan (a block from our house) so they could protect us, their grandchildren, from their own daughter. My parents split up and divorced when I was 14. By then, all of us were scarred, damaged, and broken in our own ways. I felt like a failure.

Most of my life has been spent hacking a path through a metaphorical "field of blackberry bushes" instead of walking on the cleared, well-traveled path 20 feet away. When I was desperate for interaction with people, I would get out of my self-imposed "blackberry bushes" and join everyone else on the "cleared path" – socially interacting in a positive way until I couldn't take it anymore or became disruptive. Each time I rejoined the "cleared path," an appropriate (for where I was), insightful, inspiring, caring mentor was always there to encourage me to reach up and climb out of the deep hole I had created in my beingness (emotionally, physically, psychologically, spiritually).

Most people would say I am an extrovert. That is the Leo in me – I have strong Leo traits: Center of the stage, leader, loud, stubborn, hard worker, take charge, creative, well-liked, problem solver. When I feel like I am equal to the people I am with, I am "on." But when I feel inferior, I tend to get intimidated or go "off quilter," and withdraw from everyone. I am both an extrovert and introvert – totally dependent on how I rank myself against others.

I am a bit of a loner. I have several very close, loving friends, many casual friendships, and two caring brothers, but I prefer to live alone with my cat. I want my home to be a place where I can totally be "offstage." My Leo controlling characteristics are exhausting to temper and unconsciously take over when I am around others. I am a problem solver, driver, and noticeable. The exhausting part has been regulating myself, so I fit into office and social environments harmoniously... speech, dress, quietness, consensus. In the past, it was just easier to get off the "cleared path" and go back to my "blackberry bushes" to do things my own way rather than interacting harmoniously with others.

In 2000, I went to Zihuatanejo, Mexico. I had been there before with my significant other, but this time I went there all by myself. He told me I couldn't go on vacation while he was vacationing in Thailand. I responded in a loud unkind manner, packed three 12-step books (had been attending two meetings a week for 13 years), and flew off to Mexico. I didn't have a place to stay and didn't know anyone.

While in the air, the reality of this abrupt trip set in. I didn't want to get off the plane when it landed. I found a cheap place to stay and spent the next two weeks reading and journaling... implementing the changes I needed to make so I would have the courage to leave my relationship. I returned to Seattle, packed up my stuff, and moved out. I left the "blackberry bushes" one last time and humbly crawled onto the path that everyone else travels.

I was alone and lost. I had to figure out... How to be in harmony, what I wanted to do, and how to do it. I wanted to make a difference in the world. I always have, but I didn't know what I could do. I wanted to be able to say to myself at the end of my life... "My existence was worthwhile, to the benefit of others. I served my purpose." Since I was starting over, I went back to school at South Seattle College to gain professional skills. In my second year, I joined the academic community by tutoring Beginning Spanish and Algebra, then hired on in Continuing Education.

It's 2019. I just turned 70. I'm passionate about commonsense emergency preparedness. It breaks my heart to watch TV coverage of people escaping from some disastrous event, traumatized, exclaiming they didn't know what to do, what to grab, where to go, or how to reunite when separated. All of us need written plans already in place - for mandatory evacuations, to reconnect, and to shelter-in-place for weeks without power and running water.

My introduction to emergency preparedness was as a child, way back in the 1950s. My parents designated our fruit room in Chelan, WA as our bomb shelter. Maybe it wasn't a bomb shelter... I just know my parents thought we needed a place to hide from something scary. I dreaded the thought that we could be stuck together in our fruit room because there was standing room only, my parents fought a lot, and our food supply would be a lot of home-canned fruit - mostly yuckie apricots!

Emergency preparedness was reawakened in my adult life with the appearance of 3-Days, 3-Ways preparedness ad campaigns in 2004-2005. Like many in the Pacific Northwest, I felt invincible. Hurricanes are on the east and south coasts; tornados are in the center of the US; earthquakes are in California (even though there is talk of the "big one" that would affect Washington state). I looked in my cupboards and thought, "I can make it for three days without going to the store. If I don't have enough food when something happens, I can skip eating for a couple of days." I took no action.

But the preparedness seed had been planted in the '50s and I couldn't do "nothing." I complained to a good friend about how it should be longer than 3-days - at least a week! That we should team up and change the world. We tried but we never developed anything viable.

In 2006, I saw an Oprah show on the implications of a bird-flu epidemic. The doctor (guest speaker) said we needed to be prepared to exist on our own for a full month without outside help. Hospital beds would fill, borders would close. People would avoid going out in public. We needed to be self-sufficient for a month – minimum.

I didn't have extra cash to buy emergency items & food so I grabbed a paper sack and shopped from what was in my cupboards: A roll of toilet paper; some paper towels; a bar of soap; an old brush; a few band-aids; some sandwich and garbage bags; a handful of mayonnaise, ketchup, and mustard packets; some crackers & peanut butter; a can of peaches, tuna fish, and pop; an old can opener. I put my emergency stockpile sack on a shelf in a closet. That was the beginning of my emergency preparedness efforts. I was determined to "get prepared" and worked extra jobs to earn the money for more emergency necessities.

Months later, I scraped together $400 and marched down to Costco returning home with flats of pop and water, various types of crackers, canned meat & tuna, turkey jerky, cookies, and candy. I proudly put it all in a pile on the kitchen counter and smiled every time I walked in the kitchen and looked at my additional supply of emergency food. Within a few days, I began sampling what I had purchased. I thought to myself, "I want food I like in an emergency. I wonder…"

Once I broke the seal on the giant jar of chocolate-covered caramel peanuts, of course, I had to eat every piece. I didn't know what the canned roast beef would taste like and so I opened a can. It was delicious. I couldn't help myself… I ate the other seven cans. Within 3 weeks, I had consumed everything I had purchased except for some of the crackers and the water! I was so disappointed in myself. I had to start all over again… saving pennies until I had enough money to buy more.

Lesson #1) Store my stockpile of emergency food out of sight!

My preparedness efforts were very rocky. After finally saving more hard-earned dollars, I tried it once again. I went back to Costco, and this time when I returned with my (already proven to taste good) stockpile of food, I boxed it up and put it in the garage. Over the winter, my water and beverages froze, cracked their containers, and when thawed, ruined everything else under and around them. In the summer, an infestation of bugs and critters got in the cardboard boxes containing my emergency stockpile of food and I had to throw away anything that wasn't canned goods.

Lesson #2) Figure out where and how to store stuff.

The early years of trial and error in personal preparedness were truly a disaster and extremely costly as I was living paycheck-to-paycheck. I was making costly mistakes, but I kept trying.

Several years later, I began to figure out what was in a commonsense stockpile of meals, water, first aid, and other supplies, and how to store it all. I sought out preparedness information. Purchased books and downloaded lots of lists off the Internet and ended up with piles of lists and lists and lists… but not in a format that I could easily use/reuse. I built my own lists in Excel. (That presented a whole other set of issues: Lost one Excel worksheet in a computer crash with no backup and started several lists but couldn't find the files a year later.)

Lesson #3) I need some sort of printed, bound workbook where everything is listed in one place. Printed, so I can access without my computer, power, or Internet!

In 2010, I replaced my Excel worksheets with a workbook I wrote and published (but didn't promote), <u>The Family Guide to Personal Preparedness</u>. In 2014, I decided my workbook needed a major rewrite. It was just another book like the multitudes of others that was informational but still didn't suit my needs! It wasn't functional.

Lesson #4) There is much more to preparedness than simply making lists and stockpiling food, water, and supplies.

I've done a lot of research and worked hard to create the personal emergency plan I have used for years. I took this plan, added introductions to each checklist, and wrote a new Personal Preparedness Workbook – to educate and inspire others to act. This workbook addresses a broader spectrum of emergency preparedness: Evacuation planning, reconnecting, preparedness away from home, vehicle preparedness & maintenance, home preparedness & maintenance, pets, stockpiles of meals, water, supplies, medical issues, etc. Once the checklists are filled out, they can be reused to conduct three additional Daylight-Saving Time (DST) reviews. This 2-year workbook makes it easy to figure out what's already stockpiled and what needs to be added.

Lesson #5) Need reusable checklists… to keep items and plans up to date via bi-annual reviews.

These DST reviews are essential to keep my emergency plans current. For instance, I broke my leg a couple of years ago and now I have less mobility. In my DST reviews, I realized my emergency plans had to be revised because I'm not "Super Woman" anymore. I can't lift and load the large, plastic tubs I used to store my emergency stuff. I am slowly switching out to smaller, lighter containers, which are much easier for me to load into my car in mandatory evacuations. I had to update my medical history in my workbook. My wheelchair, walker, cane, and crutches are now part of my emergency stockpile medical equipment in case I need them again.

My diet has changed over the years as I try to be less of a cookie monster and transition to more nutritious meals. As my diet changes, so does the food in my emergency stockpile. I want to simulate my normal life as much as I can in mandatory evacuations or during shelter-in-place power outages. Every DST, I swap-out/replace my emergency clothing (to match the upcoming season) and replace items that have a short shelf-life. Because my stockpile contains what I normally eat… rotating out and replacing short shelf-life food items produces no waste.

In 2010, I joined emergency preparedness committees at South Seattle College and the Seattle Colleges District. In 2013, I translated and rewrote South's Emergency Plan from a Roman numeral outline into an easy-to-read Business Emergency Action Plan that is now used at the district and by several colleges in WA state.

Through my emergency preparedness committee work at South, I was introduced to FEMA (Federal Emergency Management Agency) exercises and courses. Fascinated with how the government response worked, I continued taking courses on all aspects of emergency preparedness, response, and recovery resulting in a continuity certification from FEMA in 2014.

In 2017, I needed a Business Emergency Action Plan for my own business, Hazard Strategies. I modified and reformatted the plan I wrote for South Seattle College – to fit a private-sector business. Now, I am offering this Business Emergency Action Plan to other private-sector businesses via a 6-week live, online course.

I acquired a lot of my trial and error experience in the metaphorical "blackberry bushes." But the "cleared path" has provided the way to be a productive part of a society where I can learn, participate, contribute, and lead.

Now, I am one of the mentors on the "cleared path." I help people and businesses write and implement their plans to prepare for, safely respond to, and recover from emergencies, disruptions, and disasters. I am a best-selling author, passionate educator, motivating speaker, and successful business owner. I am actively pursuing my life purpose.

Kathleen Kent

Kathleen Kent

Kathleen Kent is an educator, best-selling author, speaker, an emergency preparedness, response, & recovery consultant. She emphasizes personal emergency preparedness for all, and workforce training to make business emergency plans actionable and executed safely.

She is the author of the **Personal Preparedness Workbook**, a commonsense approach to figure out what to do to get prepared for the smallest of emergencies and even a disaster. She also leads a course **Write your Business Emergency Action Plan in 6 Weeks** for private-sector businesses.

Kathleen's training is based on her personal efforts to get prepared at home and elsewhere. Her business emergency training stems from being at South Seattle College where she rewrote South's emergency preparedness plan and through a certification in continuity from FEMA.

Kathleen wants people, families, households, and businesses to take action to protect themselves, their loved ones, property, and companies from the disruptive events that occur.

Kathleen Kent, Owner & Founder of Hazard Strategies
Emergency Preparedness Planning for People and Businesses

The Game Changer

You can reach Kathleen at:

Linkedin: https://www.linkedin.com/in/kathleenkenthazstrat/
Web: www.hazardstrategies.com
Facebook: https://www.facebook.com/kathleen.kent.319
Contact: support@hazardstrategies.com
Phone: (206) 310-4851

To view Kathleen's Game Changer Video Interview, scan the QR Code below or click on this link: https://youtu.be/8F4nT_LdoZc

Kathleen Kent

Lessons from the 20 Yard Line
by Jamie McNaughton

There it was; the bright light at the end of the tunnel and it was calling out to me! My heart raced and a shiver ran up my spine.

I have been in "the tunnel" so many times... always filled with energy and excitement. But this felt new and I wondered what was beyond that light?

It was August 28, 2016. The bright light at the end of the tunnel was pouring in from the football field in the new US Bank Stadium; the new home of the Minnesota Vikings and host of SUPER BOWL 52 in 2018!

We former Minnesota Viking Cheerleaders had been invited to perform with the current Viking Cheerleaders for the pre-game show. In minutes, we would run out from the tunnel, onto the field and create history -- The first performance at the first NFL game at the new US Bank Stadium in Minneapolis, Minnesota!

While we waited for our signal to hit the field, I found myself surrounded by amazing women who have been part of my life for three decades; deep and loving friendships woven in the fabric of where I had been, who I was then and who I am now. We exchanged giddy smiles.

Suddenly, in my mind, I was thrown back to my first year in the field entrance tunnel at the Hubert H. Humphrey Metrodome, another piece of Vikings history in 1984. It was the first year the Vikings had fielded professional cheerleaders. It was a year of learning, trials, errors, and THAT GAME, where occasionally, I accidentally cheered for the wrong team!

All of this started that May with a surprise phone call from my high school friend Tammie.

"The Vikings are hiring professional cheerleaders. Let's try out!" she exclaimed. Tammie and I were good friends in high school and on dance line together.

Try out? I had a million reasons why I couldn't.

"No, I don't think so…" I paused. The old Jamie would have jumped "all in" but this Jamie could only ask, "how did I get here?"

I grew up in a loving home. My Dad worked his way up the corporate ladder, took time to coach our sports teams, and taught us how to play cribbage. Mom stayed home with my brother, Patrick and me. She kept us busy, including play dates with my cousins and visits to our Grandparents' bakery where we helped bag bread, frost donuts, put cookies on trays… and taste test the merchandise! She took us to church and shared her strong faith and clear moral compass. Along with my Grandparents, she encouraged us to dream big, be our own person, do the right thing, and be leaders. She always told us we could be anything if we worked hard and put our minds to it. "I know you can do it," she would say.

Every week, Mom took me to tap dance lessons. Sometimes, I didn't want to go. It was a long drive and the studio was in an old school that smelled bad. Mom was encouraging, "Come 'on, Let's go! Someday you will thank me." She offered motivation and paid me a penny for every minute I practiced. I remember the day I hit 100 minutes – that dollar was an accomplishment!

I danced in school talent shows, community events, and even won a talent contest. When the First Lady, Mrs. Nixon, visited Minnesota for a public event, I was asked to present her with flowers and say a small speech! My Aunt Collen taught me to twirl a baton and I taught a tap-dancing class to her baton students. As Colleen's Country Sun Shiners, we marched in parades, performed at nursing homes and entered baton twirling contests. In high school, I continued dancing for the Park Center Pirate dance line.

During my senior year in high school my parents separated, and the unsettling process and heartfelt pain of divorce began. I maintained my place on the Honor Roll and graduated, but my spirit was shaken. How could this have happened to my family? What does it mean? What happens now? My pretty picture of "our family" was gone.

My boyfriend at the time told me he heard my parents were separating. I completely denied it! "Where did you hear that? No, they are not!" I can still hear myself saying those words, not only to him but to anyone who asked. I was in denial.

Floundering and wanting to move on, I eagerly entered the workforce. I read self-development books and was building a successful sales career. Somewhere, I started to lose my way. I lost my focus and maybe even some confidence in who I was. Instead of staying on track, I made some wrong turns. A break-up, a new boyfriend, a new group of friends where I tried to fit in, and little-by-little, personally and spiritually I got lost.

My first wrong turn was choosing to be in a relationship that was clearly unhealthy and based on wanting to be accepted instead of appreciated. Those who loved me could clearly see it was not healthy and though they tried, they didn't really like this new guy.

Then I wandered further when I suddenly decided to spread my wings and move out of Mom's house at a time when my family was in crisis. It was a selfish decision rooted in wanting to be with whomever I wanted, wherever I wanted, especially this particular unhealthy relationship.

Control and isolation are some of the first steps toward unhealthy relationships. I was becoming lost.

Then life happened without me even knowing. At first, it was just words. Awful, hurtful, demeaning words. "Girls like you are a dime a dozen." Then came the first push, followed by the first shove, and then the first flying object. "But I wasn't being beaten," I would say to myself. "It's not that bad." It is hard to believe those words went through my head. No matter how worthless you feel, no one deserves to be treated that way. Who could I go to? By this time, my only friends were his friends, in his world. And they were not an admirable bunch.

Abusive relationships do not discriminate. Anyone is a candidate despite income, color, education, gender or upbringing. The journey is complex and difficult to understand. You cover up for them. You think you can change them, fix them, help them. That's the co-dependent part. And then you fail because the reality is, you can't change someone else. And then, you think it is all your fault. And it's not!

When people hear of abusive relationships they often say, "Why do you put up with being treated that way? Why don't you just leave?"

Do you know why? It's because we are scared, and we don't know how to leave. That is what abuse does to your mind, your spirit, your self-esteem. It strips you of your boundaries, your self-worth, and self-confidence. You forget how to stand up for yourself, you forget that you are worthy of having boundaries. And now, if you do, there may be awful consequences to pay. "How did I get here?"

Stuck in an unhealthy, abusive relationship I had no self-confidence and a big dose of low self-esteem. I was afraid, embarrassed, and disappointed in myself and my choices. I found myself hanging out with a crowd that did not fit my beliefs and dreams. And I was not safe. Feeling trapped, scared and ashamed, it seemed as if there was no way out.

My shame distanced me from my family. My faith had dwindled, and I often wondered, *How the heck did I end up here? When did I stop being me? This isn't the life I intended to live!* I felt like a twig bobbing on the surface of the water, following the current wherever it took me. Destination unknown. Well, at least I was still afloat!

As a way out of my mess, I applied for a job as a flight attendant which required a lot of travel and maybe even a relocation. I thought it would be a fun career move AND could help get me out of this relationship. I had prayed for a way out and thought for sure, this was it! Though I was a final candidate, I didn't get the job and was devastated.

Without a plan, I went back to my co-dependent ways, following whatever path grabbed me, living in a world of fear, walking on eggshells without any direction; distant from the family I loved and the dreams that I had.

That's when Tammie called. She was very persuasive and insisted we try out. Fortunately, some small spark remained deed down inside and I sent in my resume.

We arrived at the "Dome" for tryouts on June 2, 1984. There were so many people there – perhaps there was an event going on? A Twins game? A monster truck rally or a concert? There were even TV crews at the entrance. We didn't realize until we got in line -- this was all for the cheerleader tryouts! Over 600 people showed up and tried out. It was a long and grueling day that went well into the evening as the judges tried to narrow the 600 plus down to100 semi-finalists.

We learned a dance and a cheer that we performed in groups. The cheer consisted of arm and leg movements choreographed to the spelling of the word VIKINGS. We were all so nervous. I think the judges heard the word VIKINGS misspelled in every way imaginable!

We left with a note instructing us to call a phone number in the morning to hear a recording with the names of the 100 semi-finalists. Remember, this was all pre-internet! The phone line was constantly busy with all 600 girls trying to call in at once. We finally got through, and to our delight, both of our names were on the recording. A few days later, we received a letter with instructions for the final auditions the following week.

Final Auditions – Exciting! Scary! We were to come prepared with our own choreographed dance to a part of Michael Jackson's "Beat It". We would also learn a new dance and have a brief interview with the judges.

My number was called, and I did what I loved – I performed! I think I made a few mistakes, but as my Mom and dance teacher, Dorothy always said, "Just keep smiling and keep dancing." The interview immediately followed our dance. I approached the judge's table. I was completely out of breath and sweating profusely, sweat pouring down my face. I could hardly talk and was about to drip all over their paperwork! I don't even remember what they asked me. I was nervous and so thrilled just to be there. Then it was over. Time to wait... for a letter... in the mail.

It took me forever to open the beautiful envelope with the gold embossed Viking logo in the corner. I was so nervous. Would it be another embarrassment and confirmation of the little voice in my head that said I wasn't good enough?

Slowly, I tore the seam and pulled the letter out. I saw the word "Congratulations"…

That was all I needed to see. The rest was a blur. My friend Tammie's letter said the same. We were officially on the inaugural professional Minnesota Viking Cheerleading Team. The first person I called was Mom to say thanks!

We signed contracts and rehearsals started immediately. All the women had full-time careers or were full-time college students, so the grueling rehearsal schedule was added to our daily responsibilities – I LOVED IT! Our coach was an amazing, talented lady and mentor. She was a professional with high expectations; a leader with a firm yet loving manner, and she believed in us. We stay in contact to this day and I will be forever grateful for her belief in me. My confidence grew; I found new, healthy friendships and relished the intense workouts as I reconnected with my true self. Slowly, I began to move out of the current and 'swim" in my own direction.

The pre-season started and was full of fan-are. We performed at charity events, in shopping malls, and at festivals. Our first performance in the Metrodome was nationally televised!

As the season progressed, we grew confident in our game day routine listening for music cues and dancing through commercial breaks and quarter rotations. I was filled with gratitude and I choked up every time we stood on the field for the national anthem. I loved cheering for the Vikings and performing in the Metrodome for the Viking fans.

Then came December 16, 1984, a home game against our neighboring rival – The Green Bay Packers. In our locker room pre-game talk, we were reminded this was an important game for our team. The fans will be loud, there would be more than the usual camera crews on the field, and the sidelines would be crowded. Our job was to charge-up the fans and keep the excitement alive. We were pumped up and headed down to the field!

The energy from the stadium seeped into the tunnel where we waited. We could feel it. The Metrodome stands were full as we ran out for the national anthem. Dressed in purple and white, our metallic gold pom-poms sparkled as they reflected the Metrodome lights. Splashes of green and gold broke up the usual sea-of-purple throughout the seats in the stadium.

Wow! There were even Green Bay Packer fans in the crowd. As expected, the sidelines were swarming with TV crews and photographers.

The kick-off started the game and we performed our opening dances. From the sidelines, we could see the football spiral through the air but couldn't see the actual play, (this was before the technology of ginormous TV screens and instant replays). The crowd cheered and so did we.

And it was loud! You may have heard how Chicago Bears Coach Mike Ditka referred to the Metrodome as the "Roller-dome" due to the loud fans. That resulted in the Roller Blade company sponsoring us all with Roller Blades, which we wore at the next game! Great for rolling, but tough to dance in!

Cheerleaders dance when there are time outs, commercial breaks, a score from either team or anytime other time the play is paused. By halftime, the score was 21-0, (unfortunately NOT in our favor) so we were dancing a lot. And since we were behind, we were cheering a lot too. Our adrenaline soared, and the energy in the Dome flowed through my veins. I was looking forward to half-time when we would retreat to our locker room for a quick break to rest, get water, and hear feedback from our coach. I just knew it would be great.

When we entered the locker room, I anticipated glowing approval and was completely surprised when I saw the serious look on our coach's face. She gathered us together, and in her kind, but direct tone told us our energy, dances, and cheers were great. Then she said, "BUT... ladies, YOU'VE GOT TO WATCH THE GAME!!!"

We were so wrapped up in the cheering fans we neglected to peer through the crowded sidelines and focus on the actual gameplay. We were the home team on our home field with our home fans. When the crowd cheered, we cheered. We didn't consider the impact of the exuberant Green Bay Packer fans. We didn't consider they were loud and cheering too!

When we relied on the crowd, we weren't always cheering for our team! Like the twig following the current, we followed the crowd to cheer!

That was my "Locker-Room Moment". What an awakening! How foolish we must have looked, cheering and dancing when our opponents completed a pass! I was stunned. We regrouped for the second half and committed to focus on the field and on the game. We had to be cheerLEADERS and not follow the crowd!

In the second half of the game, we watched the field and cheered FOR the VIKINGS! Though our cheers did not lead our team to victory (GB-38 MN-14), from the 20-yard line in the Hubert H. Humphrey Metrodome, this Minnesota Viking Cheerleader learned a valuable lesson in cheerleading and in life. When you take your eye off the game and follow the crowd, you may not be cheering for your home team – or yourself! You are no longer creating or pursuing your dreams.

As a result of the 1984 season, I resumed being a cheerLEADER in my own life. With help from my Mom and Step-Dad and support from my brother Patrick, I left my abusive relationship. I grew stronger and strengthened my faith. I started LEADING again. My Hopes. My Dreams. My Life.

I am a huge proponent of self-development work. I dug out my old books (fortunately, most self-development principles are timeless and many of the books written decades ago are still relevant). I read, I joined groups, attended workshops, and surrounded myself with inspiring, motivated people. The Vikings organization offered tremendous support. I worked through the mindset issues that caused me to get lost in the first place. Tammie and I even spoke at our high school and shared stories about self-esteem, confidence, and cheerleading experience. Most of all, I started to believe in myself again. Investing in yourself has a multi-faceted return on investment!

For seven seasons, I had the honor to be a Minnesota Vikings Cheerleader as well as a team captain. I met lifelong friends and had once-in-a-lifetime experiences. I made a business deal that allowed me to purchase my customer accounts and start my own company which I sold five years later. My brother Patrick and I started a successful product development, manufacturing, and marketing business which we still operate today. Our products have been sold all over the world and have graced the pages of magazines and appeared on national TV shows. I know we make an impact because our products make people's lives easier, better, safer, and more fun.

I have been able to serve on the Board of Directors for several organizations including a women's shelter for victims of domestic abuse, a mediation program, and a youth peer leadership group. While cheerleading, we had the opportunity to do wonderful community work including time with our nation's veterans and in children's programs. When given the opportunity, I share my cheerLEADER story because it is relevant in business and in life. Whether you lead a team, a company or are simply trying to lead yourself – empowering your inner LEADER and having the courage to play your own game is essential to your hopes, dreams, and life.

In product development, every new product is a new game. It doesn't make sense for us to make a product that already exists. Differentiation is what gets you out of the crowd. With every new product Patrick invents, we must first make it happen, then lead and show how it is new, different, better, safer, or more fun than the other products in the market. We cannot sit in the crowd.

My husband and I met on a blind date. Greg was a successful businessman in his family's grocery business. He championed concern about the environment before that was a cool thing. He promoted organic foods in their stores even though it was at a higher cost because it was what he believed in and he knew he would find a way to make it work. He was "on the field" and that was his "Game". He taught me about the importance of recycling and caring for the environment. (This was before communities had established curbside recycling programs.) I saw a "can crusher" at a metal shop and bought it for him for his birthday (how romantic!).

This led to Patrick and me working with the can crusher company, helping communities with their recycling programs, marketing can crushers and ultimately developing an entire line of products to help "Make Recycling Easy". We got the Can Crusher into our nation's largest retailers and our entire line of recycling products into Target and Ace Hardware Stores.

Every entrepreneur knows that, beyond all the "best practices" in business, your new idea is a new game. You must step out from the crowd, get on the field and lead your way to success. Remember and embrace your uniqueness. What makes us different is what makes us great!

Everyday tweens and teens are challenged with life-impacting choices and the peer pressures that accompany them. The desire to fit in and belong can be an enticing trap to follow the crowd. Your hopes and dreams, your unique gifts, cannot shine unless you are willing to get on the field and play your game.

We all get lost sometimes. "In the crowd" can be an easy place to hide. The good news is you can get back on your field and start playing your own game. You can cheer-LEAD your way to back on track. It is simply a choice and you get to choose.

I challenge you to look at you're your biggest dreams. What are they? Are you living and cheering in the direction of those dreams? Or, have you forgotten them? Or never took the time to discover them?

You are a miracle; no one else is like you! No one looks like you, thinks like you, laughs like you. No one else has your unique gifts or purpose. Do you know your gifts? Your Purpose?

Are you hiding in the crowd? Or are you on the field in the game and cheering out loud?

We live in a time of unlimited accessibility. If you are ready to have your "Locker-Room Moment", ready to start cheer LEADING for "Team YOU", get books, find a reputable coach, online program or local group that can support you in getting out of the crowd. You get to choose.

So, suddenly, here I was back in the US Bank tunnel. Our "starter" raised her hand and shouted "Go! Go! Go!" That was our cue, it was time to dance!

As we ran down the field, we were fueled by the energy and excitement in our new stadium! (It's much bigger than the "Dome.") I am grateful and in awe of the path that led me here and my lesson from the 20-yard line of the Metrodome, where I learned the importance of playing your own game.

To be your true self, embrace your uniqueness, engage your extraordinary gifts and realize your hopes and biggest dreams – Get on the field and Be a cheerLEADER, don't follow the crowd.

Now, THAT is something to cheer about!

Three Things You Can Do Now:

1. Get complete clarity around who you are, the life you want to lead and the impact you want to have in the world.
2. Make the decision to create and live the life you want. You don't have to know how, start by making a powerful decision to create it. When you decide, you have taken the first step.
3. Surround yourself with people you admire, are inspiring and will support you. Join an inspirational, empowering group, a business organization or networking club and find a good mentor (free or hired) who can guide and support you.

Love & Cheers!

Jamie

ADDITIONAL FUN NOTES:

In 2018, I joined my fellow MVC alumni as a part of the Super Bowl Crew 52 Team. We danced as a part of the Morris Day and the Time concert on the Nicollet Mall and we welcomed football fans from around the world to our home stadium with cheer from the Bold North!

On August 18th, 2019, in celebration of the NFL's 100th Anniversary, and the 35th Anniversary of the professional line of Minnesota Viking Cheerleaders, the MVC Alumni once again join the current Minnesota Viking Cheerleaders in a pre-game performance at US Bank Stadium. We start rehearsals this week – the Tunnel is calling!

Guess who set Greg and I up on our blind date? Tammie! We are blessed with two amazing young men, Logan and Hunter, two black labs named Buddie and Rosie, and will celebrate our 25th anniversary later this year!

The original Can Crusher birthday present still hangs on the wall in our garage. Patrick and I are celebrating our 35th year in business!

A Cheerleader's Cheer
By Jamie McNaughton 1998

Keep your eye on the ball, play your own game, go after whatever you dream;

Don't be afraid that you might fall, and know things are not all as they seem.

Know your own field, make your own plays, and when the group starts to get real loud,

Remember to be your own cheerLEADER, you don't have to follow the crowd!

If you're in so deep that you can't see the game, the scoreboard is always there;

Look up past the lights and ask for guidance in saying a little prayer!

Know your own field, make you own plays and when the group starts to get real loud;

Remember God is your greatest cheerLEADER, you don't have to follow the crowd!

The Game Changer

Jamie McNaughton

Jamie McNaughton is the Co-Founder and Vice President of McNaughton Incorporated, a Minneapolis-based product development, marketing, and manufacturing company. She and her brother, Patrick founded the company in 1985 while Patrick was still in college. Patrick is the inventor and Jamie loves to connect with retailers, get their products onto store shelves and into the hands of those who need them. Together they "Create Products that Make Life Easier, Better, Safer and More FUN". Their products are sold globally through retail chains, independent retailers and online. Today, they have 9 product lines that include over three hundred clever products!

Patrick, Jamie, and their products have been featured on the Today Show, National News Stations, local and regional TV and radio, USA Today, The Costco Connection, Entrepreneur Magazine and many other national magazines and newspapers across the country.

Jamie has served as President of her local Chamber of Commerce and on several non-profit boards supporting women, youth and community programs. From the 20-yard line, cheerleading for the NFL Minnesota Vikings, she learned valuable lessons in leadership and strives to inspire others to be their best. She uses these skills every day as the "Chief Cheerleading Officer" (CCO) for the talented McNaughton team and in speaking engagements, workshops, and classes through her Life and Leadership Institute. She also coaches new product creators on how to navigate the process of getting their products into the marketplace.

Her decades of diverse experiences give her an eclectic and unconventional perspective on Business, Leadership, and Purpose that is both contagious and engaging.

Jamie and her husband Greg are proud parents of sons, Logan and Hunter, two young men who have also picked up the ambitious entrepreneurial drive to make a positive impact. Their family loves to travel together, snow ski and participate in almost anything that includes water!

Connect with Jamie at any of these websites:

www.McincShop.com
www.TidalWake.com

For Workshops, Classes or Speaking Engagements:
TheLifeandLeadershipInstitute.com

For More Info about McNaughton Incorporated:
https://www.mcincshop.com/about-us
https://www.mcincshop.com/making-a-difference
Email: Jamie@TheLifeandLeadershipInstitute.com

To view Jamie's Game Changer Interview, Scan the QR Code Below or Click this Link: https://youtu.be/poMD5kBud64

Every Roadblock is an Opportunity to Grow and Shift

by Steven Logreira

In 2010, I decided to shut down a niche business in Minnesota that had run its' course. I had to make a choice to either shut it down or restructure. Around that same time, I met a girl who was from Venezuela. She was in the U.S. on a student Visa. Once that visa ran out, she had to move back to Venezuela.

Right before she graduated, she received news that she had been granted permanent resident status to Canada and decided to emigrate. I knew she was "The One," and picturing life without her seemed unthinkable.

Unfortunately, marriage was not an option for her to remain in the U.S. because her visa mandated that she return to her native country. Venezuela was in a deep economic and political chaos and going back was not an option. So, the Canadian residency was a blessing for her and led to a life-changing decision for me.

The business I was in had literally burned me out and the idea of shutting it down was quite scary but at the same time, felt right to do so. I followed my instincts, shut down my business, paid off most of my debt, sold my house, and had a huge garage sale. I packed everything up and loaded it into a 24ft U-Haul truck and started the 1,500-mile journey to Canada with my two dogs, Black Bean and Pete in tow.

I did have two "lifelines" that I thought would keep me afloat while I settled in Canada. One was a business opportunity with a network marketing company that had just started doing business in Vancouver, and the other was a rental property that I owned which provided income that would cover my car payment and insurance; the only two bills I had left.

These "lifelines" quickly turned from something that was going to keep me afloat, to a 20,000 lb. boulder that sank me to depths I wish no one would ever have to experience. The "business opportunity" became a source of desperation that everyone I spoke to could smell from a mile away and the rental property turned into a heated dispute that eventually ended in foreclosure. My "friend" decided that paying rent just was not on his list of priorities.

Vancouver Canada is a very expensive city, so my savings ran out in a matter of months. As an immigrant to Canada, I needed a work permit to get a job and I couldn't work without a Permanent Residency Card (The Equivalent of a Green Card in America) so I was stuck.

When I finally ran out of money and had to figure out a way to make ends meet, I took whatever job I could find that paid me under the table. I did everything from junk removal, to landscaping, to building fences.

Here I was, an educated man with a degree in computer engineering, tons of work experience, and used to a six-figure income, working for $50 a day just to make ends meet. To say the least, it was very humbling, and I hit an all-time low.

What followed was a period of deep depression that almost cost me my life! Suicidal thoughts were a daily occurrence and the only thing that kept me going was that girl who became my wife. I'm not sure if I would still be here without her support and encouragement and also my strong belief in God. I found myself praying and meditating on a daily basis for things to change.

One day, I believe God answered my prayers. We were at a restaurant having lunch and I saw this magazine for a Meditation Center that just happened to be about a 10-minute drive from my house. I went to one of their weekly evening meditations and quickly realized that the place was special.

Not only did they offer something I desperately needed, but they also didn't charge for their classes and retreats. They were strictly by donation. That same night, I enrolled for an 8-and-a-half-day retreat that started the following week; somehow, I knew that this was the answer to my prayers. For the next year, I attended all the classes and free retreats they had to offer, and through that, I slowly started to come out of my deep depression and began to rebuild my life. I would in turn volunteer and give back as much as I could. That place literally saved my life!

As I began to rebuild emotionally, other opportunities for income started showing up. Talking to a neighbor who worked from home, she told me about a website called Elance. It was a place where you could find freelance work on the internet.

I always felt comfortable around technology, so doing tech work always came naturally to me. I taught myself how to use WordPress and how to build specialized websites to deliver online courses; some people call them membership sites. Since I couldn't legally work in Canada, doing freelance work on the internet was a great way to earn income and was, of course, much better than manual labor.

Once I got my permanent residency, I started to hunt for a regular job. The freelance work was bringing in money, but only enough to survive. So, I put together my resume and began the job hunt. I looked for six months and just couldn't find anything that would pay the type of salary I was used to.

To be honest, a part of me wanted to continue as an entrepreneur and not give in to finding a job. After six months, I decided to turn my freelance work into a business. I put my head down and focused on growing it.

What I learned most in this journey was that working on mindset and freeing myself from disempowering beliefs that kept me stuck was the key to my success.

One day, while I was out networking, I met an angel by the name of Kim who practiced a healing modality called "The Emotion Code." I had done other things such as Landmark, Psy Seminars and other personal development courses. Kim's work was different. She helped me release many trapped emotions that had plagued me through childhood and my adult life. I realized that I was healing some deep wounds created by childhood traumas. The more I released the better life got!

For three years I worked on myself and played what I jokingly called the

"Feast or Famine" game. I would look for a project, find it, work on it until completion, get paid and then start again.

Elance made it simple and it paid OK. Then Elance sold their company to another company called Upwork and things began to change. Upwork catered to people that were looking for "cheap" yet skilled freelance workers. I saw a drastic decrease in what people were willing to pay and it was starting to reflect financially.

Eventually, Upwork was no longer an option, and I started to study marketing and sales so that I could find a better quality of clients, clients who were actually willing to pay more for my services.

After learning how to do digital marketing for myself, I expanded the online course business into helping clients market their courses and businesses. This was a long painful journey that challenged me in ways I had never could have imagined. I was still playing the "Feast or Famine" game. Some months were great but others, not so great.

I knew I needed things to change, so I started looking for a mentor. Someone who could help me get out of that vicious cycle. Eventually, I found someone who truly helped me to begin to think about myself and my business in a new way. I absorbed his teachings and started thinking about business, money, and life in a new way.

We worked together for a few months and one day, he approached me with a business idea. He wanted to create a team and launch a course on sales which was one of the things he excelled at. After doing some market research, he realized that his specialized knowledge was in high demand and he put a team together that would make it all happen. We worked tirelessly for about three months building the marketing infrastructure to launch the course. We all worked long hours, including evenings and weekends.

The initial launch was a success! We grossed over $750K in a matter of

weeks. We were all very happy and I thought I had found what I was looking for. Little did I know that fate would dictate otherwise.

It was a Thursday evening, I tried to log-in to our back-end systems to get some work done, and my access was denied. My first thought was…`

WHAT THE HECK IS GOING ON?

I quickly called my team lead, and he dropped a bomb on me letting me know that my services were no longer needed.

I had been butting heads with one of the co-creators of the course and it affected the team, so they decided to let me go.

I was devastated, of course, and nearly collapsed into another massive depressive episode. I remember going for a long walk in the rain feeling like my entire world had collapsed AGAIN!! I got home and the next day woke up with the worse sore throat I had ever experienced. I ended up in the hospital emergency room and was diagnosed with severe strep throat. I was on bed rest for a few days, very sick and massively depressed.

I finally got over the strep throat a week later but was still depressed. What brought me back to sanity was again going back to what had worked so well; another meditation retreat and more sessions with Kim.

I was able to clear my head and began to look at that whole experience objectively. I quickly realized that my team member was right. There was a personality mismatch. I didn't fit in with that group. It was a blessing in disguise that led me to objectively look at what was working and not working in my life.

This was right before Christmas, so I chose to take the month of December off then figure out my next move.

After the holidays, I decided to use the knowledge I had learned about sales and got a job selling for a coach. I did well and it paid the bills. But it became overwhelming.

The coaches had a great marketing system that was generating a lot of leads. In turn, I was spending too much time keeping track of leads on spreadsheets and writing notes on a notebook. It eventually became a nightmare for me to sell and do all the admin work needed to not only keep track of my sales pipeline but to also generate reports for the coaches to keep them up to date with my efforts. I knew I needed to make some changes, so I went back to my tech roots and put together a system to help me keep track of the leads and easily follow up. The system was so good that I immediately started seeing results not only on the time I saved but also by being able to triple my sales.

Even though I was making decent money, I eventually began to feel as if something was missing. I wasn't feeling fulfilled.

I had a talk with a good friend, and he helped me realize that just doing sales was not fulfilling enough for me. I needed to be problem-solving and working with technology.

By this time, it was Christmas again, and I decided to quit my selling gig. I began to market my own new system that helped me get organized and properly follow up.

I again took all of December off and started talking to colleagues and other business owners about this new idea for a business. The feedback I got was overwhelmingly positive.

I quickly got a couple of clients that were interested in my system and my new business was born. Now as I write the chapter in this book, business is THRIVING!!

Since 2010, my life has changed so much! I came to realize the importance of personal development and how important it is to continuously work on my mindset. The biggest lesson was to learn to look for opportunities in what seemed like a failure and to look at every roadblock as a way to grow and shift. Most importantly, I learned to trust myself and trust God!

As long as I stay optimistic and continue to meditate and pray, I create a space to listen to the divine guidance that is always there. That guidance is available to all of us when we are willing to quiet our minds and trust in something bigger than ourselves.

I truly believe that we have the power to create our own reality. I look back at all the challenges in my life and realize that they were all growth opportunities that have led me to where I am today.

I am now committed to a life of continuous and never-ending improvement through self-awareness and consistently making changes when I need to.

To view Steven's video interview, click the QR Code below, or follow this link: https://youtu.be/1sKabm509_Y

Steven Logreira

Automation Expert- Steven Logreira

Steven is the founder of The Sales Process Mastery Course and The Sales Process Automation System (AKA The SPA System).

He is a graduate of the University of Florida School of Computer Engineering and has a minor in Business Administration. He started his career working for IBM as a Technical Sales Specialist.

As he worked with clients, He quickly realized the importance that systems and automation can have in impacting productivity and thus increasing revenue.

He has spent the last 8 years as a technical adviser in all aspects of digital marketing and has, over 19 years of sales experience.

He considers himself a big nerd and an automation expert and as well as a seasoned sales professional.

Now clients hire him to help them create their sales process and then implement a simple back-office system to automate that process and ensure that his clients save time and energy, and don't miss sales opportunities ever again.

Contact Steven
Web: http://automatemysalesprocess.com
https://www.facebook.com/Automate-Your-Sales-Process-2191061317777705
https://www.linkedin.com/in/slogreira/

-6-

Adding the Power of Faith to Your Business

By Dottie Arehart

You may have heard the concept that communication is seven percent words and the rest is equally divided between body language and tone of voice. This begins with what we have in our heads.

How do you deal with people who upset you? Are you annoyed? Do you want them to stop upsetting you, but they keep on going? Eventually, you feel yourself getting angry and you lash out at them. Then you're surprised when you get an angry response back. You make it their fault for offending you and they, no doubt, feel the same way.

I have a sign in my house; "adults get upset when you show childish behaviors." Believe it or not, six months ago, I had not yet grasped that concept. Looking at that sign each day has helped me. I try to stop allowing myself to feel like a victim. I am no longer seeking unhealthy attention for my inner child.

When a person is angry, others will pick up on that and react in a similar manner. If you are an adult and you lash out at someone, no doubt they are going to lash out in return.

The other day, I got angry because a zoom link was missing from an important email. I was mad at my teacher's assistant who was supposed to be in charge of this for not giving me the link. This caused me to miss the second call of a very expensive course that I was taking. Quite frankly. I did not appreciate this at all. I let the assistant know how I felt in a very direct manner. Her response was not pleasant; in fact, it was a very angry response to my frank disapproval. I thought I was being an adult to tell her I was displeased with her for creating this problem for me and I believe that her response was inappropriate as she is in the employ of my teacher and she dropped the ball.

In my opinion, she was disrespectful, condescending, and demeaning and it really triggered me. Somehow her words made me feel ashamed and very angry, on the verge of rage.

I am very aware of the fact that no one has the power to make you feel a certain way. I've been through enough therapy to know that when things like this happen, they often have nothing to do with the person you believe has wronged you or with whom you are angry. Rather, it's a reaction based on something that happened to you earlier on in your life. You are bringing back up an event or a feeling from your past that was hurtful. When I got so angry at this assistant, it had little to do with her or her actions. The rage was from an old wound and her reaction brought that rage back to the surface.

When I was a kid, my dad would often exhibit a great deal of rage, but I was a kid and had no ability to speak up when he behaved this way, I was too afraid of him. So, now I when try to speak up, it is often not good for me or other people in my life because I quickly turn to anger. What's happening is that I'm going through a childish phase and I know that I need to stop this kind of behavior. My lashing out doesn't make the other person feel good and it doesn't make me feel good.

I have just started a one-year course with the person this assistant works for. I love my teacher and I feel sad and upset that most of the communication I have with my teacher is through this assistant who brings out the worst in me.

So, what does this all this have to do with sales? The answer is, EVERYTHING!!!!! People will not buy from you if they don't like or trust you and believe me, they're reading you and both your verbal and nonverbal behavior. I have been studying Michael Rosenberg's course on nonviolent communication for about five years now. I love what I've learned.

I want to always be sweet, kind, and understanding. I don't want to avoid this assistant because of my current mood or method of communicating with her or because we are not in a good place in our communications. I don't want to continue to be angry and dismissive of how she might be feeling. It hurts my very sensitive heart to continue this way. I want to be a grown-up. I'm 74 years old and do not want to be considered a difficult or angry person.

I want to be a curious, warm, and kind person who gives people the benefit of the doubt. Sometimes other people are going through a difficult time or are simply having a bad day. They may be upset about something we are unaware of and they too may be acting rashly and may even regret their actions as well. I want to help people in pain, not get mad at them. I want to show sympathy and even empathy. We are all humans and we all have troubles of our own.

What I'm learning more and more regarding how to be successful in sales is the correlation between your ability to succeed and your own self-esteem. Does that make sense to you?

A person's past often affects the salesperson's ability to deal with difficult clients. Sales is a tough job and some questions are tough to ask. If you have low self-esteem you won't want to ask the hard questions. You will be afraid to be seen as too confrontational and asking certain things of a client might be scary. Your ego may be too fragile to hear the "no's."

You can't serve someone very well if you don't know what's troubling them, so you have to ask questions that address their possible pain points. Sometimes it will be hard for them to answer those difficult questions and sometimes they'll cry. That's hard to sit with but necessary for both of you. Have you heard the saying that the money is in the pain?

It's true! Think about it, most people are not going to buy unless they have pain that the purchase will alleviate. Often the person in pain is also delusional and not facing the pain because it hurts too much. After talking about their pain, sometimes they realize that their number one pain is their lack of money, or that their income is not covering their needs. You may have to ask a question regarding their budget. Can they budget the funds that will solve their problems? You will have to use a gentle and kind tone to nurture them and to help them through this difficult discussion. You may need to ask other painful questions to see if your product or service would help them.

Let me stop here to say that if you do not sell a product that is really

excellent and that you would not sell to your mom or your best friend, then find another product! If you sell something you're not proud of, every time you try to sell it you're going to lower your self-esteem more and more. Nothing is worth lowering your standards for, just to make money. It's simply selfish and unkind to sell something that is not helpful to others. God will not bless you in the long run. God made you for a purpose - your purpose is to use your unique blessings and to share with others only things that will make them happier, will improve their lives, help them and their families be less stressed.

If they cannot afford what you are selling and they really need your product or service, hang in with them and see what you can do to help them find a safe and comfortable way that they can afford it. If your product would not really work for them, move on and don't try to make a sale that is not good for them as it will not be good for you either. Consider the real-life stories that have really helped people you know, or you have worked with. Those are the stories that matter. That is the experience you should seek to have and repeat.

Clients are not stupid. They are going to pick up on it of you are being dishonest or disingenuous Selling something that's really not helpful to people is the epitome of selfishness and your potential client will see that he or she is more of a victim than a sale.

I feel great at the end of the day when I have offered a great product to someone that will sincerely help them. If they say yes, I'm psyched and excited for them. If they say no, I respect where they are in their life and hope I have served them to the very best of my ability.

Sales can really be fun *if you get the sale*, but it can be upsetting if you don't. You find yourself thinking," Shucks, I should've done this I should've done that." If you really need the sale, there is even more pressure.

If you're the only person you can depend on and you have to have a solid income, life can be really scary. You feel good when things are going well but you feel down, worried, and scared when they're not. It can be quite a roller coaster.

A fantastic option that I would like you to consider is to trust in Jesus of the Bible. It's my belief that He is the savior of the world. Having had a very unloving, mean father, it's taken me a very long time to believe in

God, a father who loves me; even takes care of me. But thanks to all my struggles these past six years, starting a new life and a new career with such hardship, I cried out to God and do now believe, and I am so grateful. I would be an absolute wreck if I didn't.

My life has changed so much since I cried out to God because of my business trials. I am so grateful for all the trials which may seem hard to believe. I feel this way because those trials brought me to the love of my Father; a Father I had never known I so needed and cried for. I had to provide for myself.

It was 2018 and I had spent literally hundreds of thousands of dollars and I still didn't think I was going to be able to make it. I began to read my Bible every day. I loved it and I still do. I don't watch regular TV anymore. When I want to watch something while I'm having lunch or after dinner, I watch Christian TV and I love it. I had been trying to learn all the things I needed to start teaching sales techniques to women. I tried a million things I had never known about before selling real estate in Virginia. Facebook, JV partnership, word.com, speaker training, business building, and putting my course online, all seemed so important and I struggled through them all still not "feeling" that I was going to succeed. But I believe this is what God wanted me to do, so, I did I and I was and still am very excited about it.

Even though I know that my product is excellent and made me rich once before, the power of fear sometimes haunts me.

In the seven years I've been in California, I've gone down many roads with many doors closing for one reason or another. Then I read a book called, *Believe Bigger,* by Marshawn Evans Daniel. In the book, the author said to find a purpose; to look at what unique things God has done for you and seek ways in which he may want to use you to help his people. It was so clear. Forty years ago, I took one course about marketing, a five-day course from 9 to 5 about sales, and what I learned made me rich.

The material was so good, and the teaching was excellent. One of my courses was about scripts and we had to practice most of the day every day from 9-5 for five full days. I came home to Virginia from Detroit and was an immediate success using their material. Within a year, I was number one or two in the number of transactions in my office and things stayed that way for almost forty years. In my prime, I sold 50 to 55 houses a year by myself without a team. Most realtors sell four houses a year.

Wow, what a blessing!

I believe that God said, "I want you to teach women the skills I blessed you with." So, that's what I do and I'm very happy about it.

I said to God, "God this is a little crazy. I didn't need any of the courses that I spent so much of my retirement money on." I felt God say, "No, but you needed to feel the pain and the hardship of starting as an entrepreneur so that you could have an understanding of the trials and stress of your students." I was happy and excited to help in an area that I had been so strong in. Today, I am teaching the system and skills that I learned forty years ago as a single mom of a three-year-old and an eight-year-old working only thirty hours a week. It was fun then.

Because, as I mentioned, it was so hard starting a second career. I depended on Jesus every day. I had to decide if I was going to honor God's word and do what He had told me to do, follow the 10 Commandments and especially have no other gods before him. I think I believed I was a little bit of my own God. I thought I could fix everything, provide everything for myself and my children. I think pride, money, and power are hard. As I look back, I had been a believer, a churchgoer, a Bible student, but I never really depended on God nor asked his help with my business. To tell you the truth, I didn't think I needed any help. I was doing far better than anything I'd ever dreamed of.

New in California, and starting a new business, I needed help! It took a very long time but finally, I have grown spiritually. In the last three years, I have grown more than I did in the previous thirty. I pray every day now. I read my Bible, and I watch Christian TV and I love it. I have learned that I have a wonderful Father who loves me (God) and He will care for me every day. If it's tough, I go back to what I believe, not what I'm afraid of. Six months before I started teaching, I had my fourth mini-stroke and was facing death. After I recovered, I said, "what do I really want to do with the rest of my life?" I figured what I really wanted to do was to teach women that they were loved by God and that they could rely on him to provide for them.

I wish I had known Jesus before. I see now it's normal to not reach out until you need God. I was lucky. I had a cushy life for forty years because of the skills and the wonderful training that I was given. But a lot of women I know are not living a cushy life and neither am I. So, I can help them know God better, rely on Him and with my TV buddy Joel Osteen, teach that God can be our champion. That is the course I use in my class. It's so much fun.

They say if you ever want to master something, teach it. I believe that's true because I'm teaching spiritual sales training and I have to be on my game and have integrity. I have to fight the fight my clients are fighting. When I'm down, scared, I have to go to God, and I come out of a funk and back in faith in God. I don't have to tremble with fear, and I have the option to believe Jesus had died for me and gave me a new life. John 10:10 says, "I have come to you that you might have life and have it more abundantly. The thief the devil comes only to steal kill and destroy I came that you may enjoy your life and live it to the fullest."

Philippians 4:19 says, "God will supply all our needs according to his riches in glory." So, I don't have to worry anymore if I work to the very best of my ability, I'm good.

Someone said to me, do you think that if you were the daughter of Bill Gates you would have to worry about money? The answer is of course, no. The truth is, your Father in heaven is much richer than Bill Gates so, you don't need to worry and that's the truth!

The main thing that God wants from us is our faith. He doesn't need our help, He doesn't need me to help the women that I meet, but He can use me, give me a job I would love that would bless other women and make my children proud of me again.

Hebrews 11:6 says, "without faith, it's impossible to please God." When we can see and understand something, it is not faith but reasoning. Doing is doing God's will quietly and leaving the results to Him in faith.

The definition of faith is trust, belief, confidence, conviction, credence, reliance, and dependence. So, if I'm selling my service or product and have done my best with my skills and have faith in God that He will provide as He says He will. Philippians 4:19, "my God will meet all my needs according to His riches in glory."

To wind it all up in one long verse. "Do not be anxious about anything but in every situation by prayer and petition with thanksgiving present your requests to God. And the peace of God will transcend all understanding and will guard your heart and your mind in Christ Jesus." This was written by Paul in prison. Imagine. The life of faith is filled with constant challenges to become more Christlike and become our true selves.

It is not easy, but it is so worth it.

Dottie Arehart

Dottie Arehart is a speaker, seminar leader and an expert in connection with people. In her book "Getting to YES for Women." Dottie reveals her secrets from 40 years of being "tops" in her field of sales. Now at age 74, she shares her secrets of what helped her be in the top 20 of 15,000 realtors in Northern Va.

She was A 29-year-old single mom with two children ages three and eight. Six months after starting work she took three courses that, as she says, made her a star in sales for 40 years, and now she wants to pass on those secrets to other women.

Dottie, a former cheerleader, is a girl's girl and she is passionate to now have the time to give her all to teaching women entrepreneurs and professionals to get "yes", when they make an offer.

She is a very committed born again Christian and will be inner-winding sales skill with faith in God.

This book will give you new ideas and thoughts that WORK so you can experience more success in less time.

View Dottie's video by scanning the QR Code below or following this link: https://youtu.be/YcbQvn989MY

Undrownable

By Sarah Lawrence

Water is powerful. It can look calm and beautiful one moment and the next, strip us of life. We don't need water, though, to feel like we're drowning, slipping under deeper and deeper, unsure if we'll ever catch our breath again. I've spent much of my life feeling like that, constantly struggling. It wasn't until I learned to let go that I could truly live.

When I was five, I started swim lessons. I remember holding onto the side, dangling in the pool. I knew water could be dangerous and it was my responsibility to stay safe.

"Take a deep breath, let go, lie back and relax," my instructor said. "You'll float like a boat." And I did! I learned to trust my body and the buoyancy of the water.

By seven, I had mastered most basic strokes, manipulating the water in orchestrated movements. I gained confidence taking a breath, letting go and building my relationship with water, always respecting its power.

At age eight, I competed on a swim team. I remember every swim meet, every stroke as I moved smoothly and efficiently across the pool. At the end of each lap, as my hands touched the wall, I would flip and push off back toward the other side. I felt satisfied, complete and safe knowing that wall was waiting. The endless practice laps in the calm water gave me a calmness too.

As a teenager, I was flooded with uncertainty, insecurity, and chaos. One day I woke up and the calmness I had grown accustomed to was gone. My brain filled with noise that I couldn't quiet, like a radio I couldn't turn off. Some days the radio was so loud I couldn't hear my own thoughts. Other days it was a repetitive song that distracted me from living. It became nearly impossible to move through life let alone relax.

What I didn't realize then was that the noise was chronic anxiety. My mind constantly vibrated with 'what ifs,' worst-case scenarios and lies. Unlike water's calmness, anxiety's constant chaos loudly drowns out all but its own lies making even the strongest person wonder if its irrational demands are the right path. Anxiety insists that every situation is life or death, and panic is the only solution to stay alive. I desperately needed to escape the noise. I remembered the water. As I dove into the pool, the calm water caressed me, and I knew I could drown my anxiety in its peace. I could trust it and myself again.

In my mid-teens, I worked summers as a lifeguard. I was comfortable in my job and loved being around the one thing that made me happy. I was confident and able to live with a certain stillness.

One blazing day, the sun's heat reflecting off the pool was the perfect excuse to live in the water. Its blue color reminded me of the horizon where the sky and the ocean kiss. The subtle ripples in the pool called my name and I jumped in, letting the calm wash over me, just what I needed.

Suddenly hands on my shoulders pushed me deeper and deeper into the water. For a moment, my brain raced with the realization that one of my co-workers was trying to drown me. He was my age and struggled at home. He felt alone, scared, all the negative emotions that cause pain. He felt so much pain that he needed me to hear, see and feel it too. In the water, I was an easy target. His hands sought every part of my upper body they could find to push down.

My lungs begged for air. My body thrashed in a flurry of waves at the water resisted my erratic attempts to break free. As I quickly used my limited reserve of oxygen, I began to succumb to the water's stillness. I wasn't giving up. I was trusting the power in the water which could kill or save me.

My instructor's words came back to me. "Let go, lie back and relax." I did and at once slipped from my tormentor's grasp. I quickly kicked to the surface. I filled my lungs with air, a breath of life shot into the death creeping to claim me. Though water can kill, this time it saved me when I realized letting go wasn't giving up.

But we aren't fish. We can't live in water. As an adult, I feared I was only a moment away from my anxiety drowning me. Some days it manifested as rage, but I couldn't express why I was angry. Other days I cried but couldn't say why I was sad. Still others I was so apathetic that it scared me how little I cared. I felt hands stripping away my calm, pushing me deeper into darkness. In my mind, I couldn't relax, kick to the surface and breathe.

For the next thirteen years, every day I struggled for breath only to sink deeper, drowning a little more in my chaotic mind. I relived my early experience in the pool, but since I couldn't relax and let go, I grabbed onto anything and anyone I thought could save me.

At twenty-nine, I thought my alcoholic, abusive husband could save me, but he only made my struggle worse. He provided just enough "air" to keep me alive but not thrive. After eight years of his "hands" holding me under, I relaxed and let go, trusting myself enough to do what I needed to do. I left.

I thought I had finally escaped the outside force drowning me. That's when my anxiety plunged me into even darker uncertainty, filling my mind with lies. My own mind was trying to drown me.

"You aren't good enough. No one will love you." The mantra played over and over.

I begged to hit rock bottom where, like in a pool, I could push off and rise up to the air. But the bottom never came. I drifted deeper into a darkness where the chaos of my mind got louder and my fears stronger.

A year later, I met a man, Steve, who jumped into my water not to hold me down but just to be with me in my darkness. He reminded me that the power of water could bring calmness and peace and that air and light waited for me at the surface if I chose that direction.

"Don't listen to him. He'll push you back down," my anxiety screamed. "There is no peace anywhere. Stay in the dark that you know."

The lies convinced me... again. I tried everything to get this man to leave me, but he refused to let my anxiety drag me down. He didn't force me toward the surface. He provided encouragement, a positive option to my fears.

"Let go of what doesn't serve you," he offered. "Hold tight to what does and you'll leave your darkness and rise to the surface and the air you need to breathe...and live."

I was terrified, but this man helped me trust myself. I looked at the negative behaviors I was acting on out of fear of drowning. I released them and left them in the darkness. I looked at the healthy behaviors giving me breath. I embraced them and found the peace of water that buoyed me to the surface and allowed me to flow around any obstacle in life. I refused to ever again be held down, pushed under into the darkness. I chose to be undrownable.

Like water, life is powerful. It moves us forward constantly and consistently toward the special person we can become. Ignore the lies of anxiety. Let go of who and what push you down and under. Choose who and what lift you to the surface and fill your lungs with life. I did and never looked back.

To view Sarah's Game Changer interview, Scan the QR Code Below or click this link: https://youtu.be/adFllMJIKgg

The Game Changer

Sarah Lawrence

Sarah is a professional speaker, writer, and coach. Her main focus is guiding entrepreneurs on how to create a more effective space for team development, and business relationships. She has developed relationships with other coaches, consultants, and speakers that have resulted in over 300 successful business opportunities, by teaching people how to become the best versions of themselves.

Sarah was a teenager when she had her first anxiety attack. Of course, as a teenager, it was hard to label the noise in her head. It took many years to realize to toll anxiety would take. However, it was through this realization that she was able to hack her brain, reverse engineer her behavior, and learn exactly how to communicate to those around her, in a way that created a space for healing, and love.

Sarah bases all of her relationships, and career based on the idea that when you can meet someone where they are, have unconditional trust that what they tell you is their reality, and love unconditionally, you can fundamentally change life and business. Ultimately, Sarah believes that when businesses and relationships are fundamentally based in a place of trust, they become much more successful.

Instagram @Superstarupgrades
Facebook SarahLawrenceSpeaks
Sarah@Sarah-Lawrence.net

Sarah Lawrence

Disrupting the Status Quo:
Changing the Rules of Business

By Catherine Rocheleau

Did you know that 85% of workers globally, whether at the top of the company or the bottom, hate their jobs?[1] In a world where our jobs take up one-third of every working day, doing what you are passionate about is a rare gift. From the time I started my career, it has delivered both exciting opportunities and those I've hated. My goal now is to only be a part of the 15% who love what they do.

Before it was an accepted characteristic of millennials, I transitioned from position to position every two to three years. I would start each position with excitement around the possibilities that lie ahead, then, I would implement the solutions for the challenges I identified. Once I reached those goals, I would feel a great sense of accomplishment. However, if the next big challenge was absent, I became bored and had to look for new roles as each company I worked for tended to be small or medium, and internal promotions were only possible unless my boss left. With each transition, I took on more responsibility, new challenges and opened new doors.

While in my last senior executive role, there was a voice in my head reminding me, "Catherine, you are making good money and doing great things." My head told me to be happy, yet in my heart there was something missing. I was disillusioned, frustrated and constantly looking for more. This led to my decision to enter the world of entrepreneurship. I knew it was the right direction for me because it included opportunities to work in diverse areas, to learn and grow from project to project while

---

[1] State of the Global Workplace – Gallop 2017

transitioning from one client to another. What could be better than following my passion? That's what all the gurus tell us!

Entrepreneurship offered me the chance to do what I love to do. Like any job, there are some duties I enjoy more than others. Although long hours are needed at times to create the results I wanted, I have always found ways to fuel the fire within.

Obviously, there have been ups and downs, however, I have never wanted to go back to working in a "j-o-b". Being an entrepreneur has offered me opportunities that I could never have imagined doing, learning new skills and creating results for my clients that made me extremely proud. I felt like I was following my North Star, doing what I'm meant to do.

Five years ago, after being an entrepreneur for 18 years, I was feeling somewhat unfulfilled. Although I was working with great clients, and doing interesting work, I could feel the disillusionment sneaking in along with a familiar yearning for something more. But I didn't know what that "something different" was. It felt like déjà vu all over again which was troubling for me. I didn't have the passion fueling me or a deep connection to my work anymore. I wasn't engaged in my business at all – something had to change!

This realization was the beginning of a downward swing and a period of questioning myself, my work, and my vision for the future. Every question I had led to more questions and yet, answers evaded me. The big underlying question was – what did I have to do to revive my passion so I could love my work again, where I could create amazing results for my clients and grow my business?

Then, without notice, my life fell apart. I was attacked in my own home by someone I knew. This traumatic event was so far outside what I thought could ever happen to me, it left me broken in more ways than one. I had a lot to focus on, both physically and mentally. I was devastated and unable to manage my health or business effectively, so I had to make a choice – I walked away from my business.

Every day was a challenge. It felt like life's obstacles, which under normal circumstances would have been manageable, seemed insurmountable. I was at the end of my rope and could feel myself spiraling downward. It was terrifying, and I had no idea how to stop it.

Over the course of six months after the assault, not only had I lost my primary source of income, I also faced significant life hurdles. There were major repairs needed in my home, I had two flat tires in three weeks, my laptop died, my sister moved across the country, and my beloved cat passed. Each incident felt like a continuous kick to my gut. On top of that were health-related costs for treatments and expenses in my life that were now draining my savings. I was doing all I could to keep a clear head, but I was overwhelmed and exhausted.

As I struggled with my day-to-day situation, I held on to an inner desire to "return to normal". No matter how hard it got, I was not going to let one negative incident stop me from returning to the great life and business I had built. I didn't know how I would get there, or what I would do, but I was determined.

Looking back over this time in my life, I have no idea how I was able to hang on to that sliver of hope, but I am so grateful that I did. It was the lifeline that helped me stand back up and move forward. My family was my rock, providing encouragement, a non-judgemental ear when needed, financial support to bridge the gap plus so much more!

Outside of my family, few people knew what had happened to me beyond a surface explanation. Those who did know, offered gems of advice and support at the right time, helping me take the necessary baby steps I needed to keep going.

When I started feeling ready to step back into my normal life, I had big questions I needed to answer. When would I be able to get back to work and what would I be rebuilding? Would I rebuild my business, or would I get a job? Would I still work in the same area of expertise or move in a new direction? Would I still live in Vancouver or move to Victoria? Would I stay in my house or move to a new place? The number of considerations and quandaries continued to pile up.

After looking through several job ads, it became evident to me that I did not want to walk away from entrepreneurship and the business I had built over the previous 18 years. Finding a job seemed like the easiest path that would have certainty and financial consistency, which can be a challenge at times in entrepreneurship. However, with every job posting I reviewed, I didn't experience any excitement or passion. I could not imagine myself reporting to an office every day to fulfill someone else's dream at this stage in my life. The steady paycheque sounded wonderful, yet without passion, I'd just be returning to that collective 85% of unengaged and unhappy employees. This did not provide a positive outlook for me, so the decision was made – I needed to continue on my path of entrepreneurship.

After having such a successful business for so many years, it was daunting to start from scratch again. However, this was my new reality. When I realized this, I knew I needed to decide whether to return to what I did before or if I should pivot my business and head in a new direction.

Opening up to this self-exploration wasn't the easiest process but it enabled me to clearly identify what I did and didn't want. Going back through my files I found a draft of some website copy I had written years ago. I was struck by my perspective regarding connecting our heads and hearts in business. This was a lightbulb moment as I read my old copy. The awareness of sustainable development and business practices that create positive social and environmental change was very important to me – even more so now. Social responsibility (otherwise referred to as CSR in the 1990s) was instrumental in the creation of my MoreThanGreen™ program for my business in 2007. I believe when individuals and business owners look after each other, our communities and ourselves, we integrate head and heart into our calling, which creates more impact on others and positive outcomes for our business too.

Over the last 10 to 12 years, I had moved from having only a few social responsibility efforts in place to fully embracing social responsibility. I also better understood how business could really create positive change in the world and not just be a money machine. Don't get me wrong. I strongly believe that businesses need to be profitable. I also believe not-for-profits need to generate more revenue than their expenses. Without these profits, organizations are unable to grow and their ability to create a positive impact is constrained. The more a business can make, the greater the impact it can achieve.

I knew I wanted to champion businesses to adopt this opportunity, allowing them to create a lasting positive impact through their enterprise. I was tired of hearing about organizations who create profit while destroying communities, use and abuse the environment solely for profit, or made decisions with no consideration of the impact on the people in their organization. The same people who had helped them become successful.

I'm sure you have heard of the worker who has been terminated just weeks before full retirement, just so the employer doesn't have to provide a pension. What about companies that demolish houses after evicting the tenants only to leave the land empty for years? What about the businesses that cut corners only to cause a work accident or environmental catastrophe, which could have been prevented with proper precautions and regular maintenance?

As I mentioned, I created my MoreThanGreen™ program to reflect my approach to business in 2007. It is based on the triple bottom line philosophy, which drives my company's efforts to consistently deliver on our promise to be a great business partner, a great citizen and simultaneously be environmentally responsible. Ignite Leadership International® annually donates 2% of its top-line revenue to charity, and we donate our time and expertise to business groups, student initiatives, and community organizations as well every year.

The triple bottom line consists of three factors: people (workers in your company, the local and global community, your shareholders), planet (environmental factors), and profit. In the early 2000s, the green movement was top of mind. Since money is green and the environment is green, the missing element was people. Since my business was about the people, the name MoreThanGreen™ seemed fitting.

As I explored my interests, skills, and goals as well as the market, and what my competitors were offering, I knew there was a gap. Those who were talking about creating an impact were positioning it in a way that you, the business owner, would be the beneficiary, with no external benefit to the world around you. Others were promoting heart-centred, purpose-driven businesses, but profitability was low on the priority list. In some models, profit was a negative. Others still delivered the traditional profit-driven model – maximize profits at all costs, full-stop.

Very few companies were offering services to support businesses in adopting the triple bottom line model. Yes, companies are dabbling in social and environmental impact, but most are not effective in integrating these measures into their core operations. Some people refer to these front-facing efforts as a public relations stunt – tugging on your emotions so you will buy from them without looking behind the curtain.

Consumers today are becoming more discerning with their pocketbooks. They are demanding companies be more than just profit-generating machines. Using their purchasing power, consumers are choosing to buy from businesses that are more environmentally sound, who treat people well and contribute to local or global communities in a meaningful way. At the same time, employees are also selectively choosing to work for companies that have a purpose beyond just making profits. They want more flexibility, better overall compensation packages and want to be aligned with the purpose of the company's values and cultural climate.

Based on the information I gathered, I had to explore this idea further. I knew I had the skills and passion to fill this gap. The journey took me down the path of helping businesses shift towards fully integrating the triple bottom line approach. In the end, it would provide a triple win for their people, their profit and the planet.

A new classification for organizations keen on this approach allows them to become a certified B-Corporation. The non-profit organization known as B Lab defines certified B-Corps as "businesses that meet the highest standards of verified social and environmental performance, public transparency and legal accountability to balance profit and purpose." In other words, these businesses use profits to create a greater good for people in their organization, the community, and the environment. They are leaders driving a new movement using business as a force for good.

This new approach for businesses to lead beyond profit production, with the underlying philosophy of sustainable and ethical business practices, resonated with me. This ignited my passion for my business once again. It would allow me to build on my MoreThanGreen™ program and create a lasting impact on the world. My own legacy. The people I met within this community were heart-centred, passionate and focused on the mandate to do good through business. They were leading and growing businesses that were successful financially created great work-places where people thrived and clearly demonstrated the impact they were making in the world. Integrity and transparency was refreshing!

My lightbulb moments repeatedly burned brighter the more I learned. I knew this was where I wanted to be. It was the light at the end of a very trying and traumatic tunnel. I took courses, read books, attended webinars and conferences, then started integrating more and more impact initiatives in my business with increasing success.

Today, this passion has become a driver for my organization and the work I do with my clients. I know I'm on the leading edge – a disruptor to the traditional business model. Yet, the IMPACT Business Spectrum (as I've coined the transitional path for businesses) is a process that allows businesses to shift from the traditional profit/shareholder focus to a more all-encompassing shareholder focus where people, profit and planet are considered in all business strategies, decisions, and operations.

Now that I have set my direction, I am embracing the challenge to create a better world through business with these three A's, "Align, Activate and Advance". This reflects my mission: helping businesses align social impact with their existing operations, activate all of those initiatives and strategies in a profitable way, and advancing their business along the spectrum, creating a lasting legacy where their business is a force for good and leaves the world in a better place.

As we embrace a world where every workplace supports its employees to grow and thrive, each business has an opportunity to create a positive impact in their community and the environment. If we can all come together in this respect, prosperity can be granted to everyone and the planet as a whole.

No matter what stage of business you are at, or how far along the IMPACT Business Spectrum you wish to travel, I know my company can be the right partner to get you and your business delivering on your IMPACT goal.

Walking my talk in 2018, I proactively began the process to get my company certified as a B-Corp. Becoming a certified B-Corp is another way we are striving to balance our purpose, values, and profit while having a positive and measurable impact on the world we live in. And we help other businesses to do the same

.

The passion I have for this new direction ripples throughout my entire life. Imagine a tiny drop of water creating a ripple effect in a body of water. As more droplets hit the water's surface, the ripples grow and are more disruptive to the status quo. Just like the water drop, the impact I bring to the business world may start small but will grow as more businesses join me to create waves.

Together, we can change the rules of business to create a movement that will impact the world.

Catherine Rocheleau

Catherine Rocheleau

Catherine Rocheleau is a Vancouver-based passionate social entrepreneur and founder of Ignite Leadership International®.

As a leader and disruptor navigating the new world of impact business, Catherine leads clients through their Impact Business Spectrum™ journey to create profitable businesses, and great workplaces in order to reduce turnover, attract loyal customers all while creating a positive difference in the world. Her MoreThanGreen™ program underpins all aspects of her business as she advances it to become a certified B-Corp. Ignite Leadership donates 2% of top-line revenue to charity every year.

Catherine's strengths in organizational change, leadership, communication, team dynamics, and social responsibility have been developed through her rich and diverse background in the food services, healthcare, education, business, and non-profit sectors.

Catherine is an award-winning, best-selling author, international speaker, trainer, business strategist, and executive coach. She is the creator of the online program: IMPACT Business Blueprint, and host of business mastermind programs.

As a speaker, Catherine's customized talks inspire her audiences to take action, follow their passion, and be a leader of change. When not working, she can be found with her family and friends, travelling, exploring real estate opportunities, watching hockey or relaxing with a glass of red wine.

Connect with Catherine
Web: igniteleaders.com
Instagram: Instagram.com/igniteleadership
Facebook: facebook.com/catherine.rocheleau
LinkedIn: linkedin.com/in/igniteleadership
Twitter: twitter.com/ignitesolutionz

To view Catherine's Game Changer Interview, scan the QR Code below or click on this link: https://youtu.be/uvwuvivzVRY

Catherine Rocheleau

Depths of Possibility

By Jenny Murphy

I've seen the depths of the earth.

While mountain climbing in Bolivia, Mexico, and Nepal, which can include walking across vast expanses of land, often covered in snow or ice, having to jump across a crevasse, a large crack in the earth, was unavoidable. The mountain guides and Sherpas would say last year it wasn't there.

You come to the edge of the fissure in the earth, look down, and are overtaken by the darkness, the bottomless pit. But sometimes, instead of blackness, there is a mystical beautiful clear blue with light shining, a way out, sunshine from somewhere.

You have absolutely no choice. Your body is sweating underneath all the layers from the rigorous hiking and climbing, but your toes and hands are freezing. You are attached to your rope team, you cannot retreat, and you have to trust and go for it.

You step back, take a running leap, use all your strength, heavy pack on your back, sharp-pointed steel bottom boots, and you fly up and over. The other side. You've made it to the other side.

What a mystery. The endless possibilities of the earth, changing, from year to year, in the same place, a new crevasse, from shifts happening from deep within, and discoverable only with an adventurous spirit and taking that risk of the unknown.

This is the way I view the human body: endless possibilities, always moving, vibrating atoms and cells, like the malleable planet, able to change.

If you've experienced pain, you know that each pain-filled moment can be different. Some pain seems endless and dark. But some have the feeling of a mystical clear blue light coming through, a sign of possibility, like the mountain crevasse, with no visible bottom, but revealing just maybe a breakthrough to sunlight, a sign of the end of the seemingly bottomless depths of darkness.

My journey of back pain started in college. There were long hours of me and my viola alone in the practice room, perfecting techniques required of high-level classical music. Symphony rehearsals had hours of sitting with repeated motions and no options to shift physical position.

I remember feeling the pinch between my shoulder blades, an extremely tight neck, aches in my low back, stiffness, and also at times sharp pain. One traumatic memory is the day while driving as a graduate student, from school to a gig. I tried to turn my head to see to switch lanes, but my tight painful neck did not allow it. I was forced to continue driving straight in that lane until I could see from the mirrors that I was clear to move. This was the moment I realized my life had become painful and out of control.

My overbooked schedule of school plus work was insane. At 25 years old, I was in a lot of pain and too busy to deal with it. I did not know what to do and did not know of any resources to turn to for help. Even with all these challenges, the one thing I knew was that I loved playing my viola and wanted to find answers on how to overcome the pain of it.

My pursuit of back pain relief really started when I decided to move across the country about a year after finishing my Masters in Viola Performance. At the time, I had actually had a super cool life, my own apartment, teaching music in the afternoons at a music school down the street, riding my bike or hiking in the mornings, and leisurely making homemade soups and bread.

I could have just kept my simple little life. But I wanted to study with a teacher I had in undergrad who I remembered as having addressed the physical set up to the instrument. Pain, physical or emotional, can be a great motivator. When you know you have to do something, you go for it, and the details find their way.

I said goodbye to my private music students and gig colleagues, gave away my furniture, and with only my basic things packed in my awesome old green Chevy Blazer and bike roped to the top, I set out, ready for a major life change.

I drove for three days, including through an ice storm in St. Louis. I had no home address to write down on the forms at the hotels, I had barely any money and I had no real plan, except to study with the viola teacher across the country.

I found a house in the mountains where I rented a room and a job working 30 hours a week at a tea company. Every evening I spent 3-4 hours working on re-associating my body with the viola by creating my own made-up exercises. This process included sitting meditation of sorts, calming my mind and body and nervous system, then bringing my viola to my body, first on my lap, then slowly working up to the playing position, and eventually playing easy long tones to start.

Making time to hike on mountain trails a few times a week was also a priority. Mind clearing through being in nature and physically moving have a direct impact and big-picture benefit for decreasing pain and are non-negotiable aspects of my schedule as part of a healthy and fulfilling life. During this time, I also started taking weekly lessons from the viola teacher. After 6 months of taking lessons with her, she said she could no longer teach me privately as a non-college student, and since I already had a Master's Degree, it seemed the next logical step was to enroll in the Doctoral Music Program.

Research is a natural part of many doctorate degrees, so there I was taking a required research class. While others were writing dissertations on Bach melodies, quite different from my fellow classmates, the topic I chose was "Musicians Wellness: The Psycho-Physiology of Musicians".

With the specific goal of finding books on different modalities, natural methods of pain relief that musicians could use to write about in my 30-page research paper, I went to the public library. This is where I found my first book on acupuncture by chance. It felt like it was the best thing that ever happened to me. In one sitting, I read the acupuncture book cover to cover that day; it just made sense to me.

Crazy thing, later that week, I was searching the phone book for the address of a school I was to teach music. It is then I saw "Acupuncture" listed under Schools. What a coincidence! Soon, I visited the nearby school of Chinese Medicine and had some treatments. I could not believe that my pain was gone, from a few acupuncture and cupping treatments, for the first time in years.

I've always been therapeutically or medically minded. Therefore, it made sense to me that I was taking pre-med science classes simultaneously while enrolled in the Doctoral of Music program. I was planning to get a Doctorate in Music *and* Medicine (MD). In fact, one of the books for my paper was authored by someone with both of those doctorates. But I could see some disparity with this direction that was including western (regular) medicine because I had a personal library of books at home about *Natural* Medicine.

The book I accidentally stumbled upon on that fateful day in the library had allowed me to understand and receive relief from acupuncture treatments. Within months, I had enrolled in Chinese Medicine School.

Now, after years of treating patients and learning their stories and making observations, I've developed a method for people to also help themselves, much like how I figured out ways to re-associate my body with the viola to decrease the physical impact of playing it.

Recently I put my own methods to the test when I hurt my back. I'm sorry to say it was under these circumstances, but traveling to attend my mother-in-law's funeral, we had to take our 3 big dogs. I feel it's important to acknowledge that it was a stressful time because I have observed that at times of more mental or emotional pain there's a propensity for more physical pain to occur. At the hotel, the high bed was a long jump down for the oldest dog. She was hesitating, walking back and forth. Seeing her so frightened to jump down, I just picked her up and placed her down gently on the floor. Her 80 pounds and the awkward slow bending overturned out to be an injury-causing situation.

Immediately after placing her on the floor, a pain shot through my back. I slowly tried to stand upright, but the pain kept shooting through my back, I felt stuck like I couldn't move, and I had to stay hunched over. Realizing that I was not able to stand up straight, my training as a Yoga

Teacher kicked in and I proceeded to slowly and with approximation do some Yoga movements and slightly stretch my back. I also applied some acu-points that I know from being a Physician of Oriental Medicine.

Within a few minutes, I could tell the difference in the level of pain. Even after a few days, my back still had some pain, but each day I made sure to apply some techniques that I knew and not to let the pain keep me sitting. The hardest part of recovery is starting. When you are in pain it can be extremely hard to move. But knowing the benefits of even small actions, I knew I would be thankful for my efforts.

In addition to stretches and acu-pressure points, I also applied some mind-set ideas. These can also be known as affirmations or positive thinking. These mind-set ideas fit into the category of Neuroplasticity which is retraining the brain to create new neuronal pathways, different pathways in the brain where the body is not experiencing pain. You do this by thinking new thoughts on purpose.

Within a week of applying the trio method of simple yoga stretches, acu-points and mind-set I was feeling normal, strong and flexible again.

Keep in mind, if you choose to think a new thought one time but you do not feel better, remember the mountain.

When a stream is coming down from the mountain top, it follows the same path over and over, the path of least resistance, between the rocks and trees, into natural paths that are already there. As it flows in the same groove repeatedly, the crevasse gets deeper. This cycle continues, until!... there is an outside force that creates a new path.

For the mountain, an outside force could be an avalanche, extreme weather, an earthquake, or human activities such as digging a new hiking path or moving rocks.

For the brain, an outside force is your own purposeful thoughts. You can change the neuronal path in your brain that has been created by having pain. The electrical currents of neurons in your brain that have been traveling that brain pathway of your pain over and over can be influenced with your intentional thoughts to a new neuronal path that does not have the connection to your body pain. This technique is measurable, proven and is part of the study of neuroplasticity in the science community. Adding this mental practice to a physical practice like stretches to help your pain is another level of self-care in helping yourself decrease your own back pain.

Before I ever heard the neuroplasticity, I had a personal experience of getting rid of pain through intentional thinking. I worked at a doctor's office as an Acupuncturist. One day as I was drying my hair before going to work, I turned my head, felt a weird twinge, and then pain. My neck felt stiff for a couple days. Soon, I was having numbness in my thumb when I reached out my arm. Eventually, the symptoms of pain, numbness and tingling became constant.

I received treatments of Acupuncture and cupping, massage with essential oils, and also laying on a biomat. They all helped, but I was still having symptoms.

Trying to come up with ways to deal with my pain and symptoms, I remembered a meditation class I had attended months prior. In the class, one of the participants said that they had back pain from sitting there for the duration of the class. The teacher told the man to close his eyes and listen, so we all did. She started talking to the man's pain, telling the pain that it was not needed, and it served no purpose. After a few minutes of saying these things, the teacher asked the man if he still felt the pain. He paused, then said, "Uh, well, no, it is gone".

One night, I was feeling the hand numbness and neck pain that I'd

been having for a couple of months now. I was thinking about the meditation class, and how the teacher instructed the pain to go away. After trying so many types of treatments and not having full relief, I felt like I had nothing to lose and just decided to try it. I told the pain that it was not serving me anymore. I was really done with the pain, and the pain could go away. I said these words to myself over and over until I fell asleep. I also felt the words strongly because I was really ready to be done feeling this pain.

I woke up the next day feeling different. I did not know what to expect, but the results shocked me. The pain was gone. My whole body felt lighter, I felt in control, and I felt free. I was ecstatic. I will never forget how profound that felt.

Pain cannot always be avoided. Injuries, accidents, daily life, and repetitive work motions can all cause pain. There have been many cumulative events in my life that caused me to experience back pain. When I was a baby, I needed braces on my legs to keep them straight. This was because I was born with my body folded and my hip muscles were excessively tight. Because of these braces, I never learned to crawl normally. Instead, I always dragged my legs behind me. Just to connect that with my life today, anatomically, tight hip muscles will absolutely contribute to back pain.

Before I moved across the country to study the viola with the specific teacher, I was in a car accident where my car was totaled. The impact was so strong that my viola was propelled from the back seat into the dashboard. I had severe whiplash and was left with my head strapped to a flat board in the ER for three hours. This may have contributed to a long-term negative effect on my neck, back, and spine. I have also had two bad mountain bike accidents. One gave me a big scar on my forehead from 24 stitches where my headlamp cut into me when I was thrown over the handlebars. The other left me with a metal plate and 8 screws in my left arm as well as a broken tooth. I believe that wearing my helmet saved me from worse results. In addition, two long term career activities, playing the viola and standing over patients for several hours at a time doing treatments, have both been sources of back pain for me at times.

My back pain was the main catalyst in leading me to become a Certified Yoga Instructor. Previously, I had tried yoga on and off for over 20 years and generally found it to be too difficult or uncomfortable. It was at this time that my sister had made a 10-minute yoga video for a project. She's pretty advanced. I thought "there's no way I can do this".

So, it took me a year to even try. At that time, I was having a lot of back pain, so I figured I had nothing to lose. This little yoga icon was on my phone staring at me. I finally decided to take the leap and I pushed the button. I pressed play, listened, watched and followed the directions. I promised myself I would do this every day. After three days of following the yoga directions on my phone, I could not believe how much better I felt.

I was now convinced of how easy it was to quickly change my body pain through yoga. I learned not to be afraid of yoga. I realized I did not need to go to a long class with strangers and open myself to potentially feeling embarrassed, to get benefit. Learning how to help yourself when you are feeling pain can change your life.

Living life fully, being in the breathtaking mountains, feeling the meditative focus that hundreds of rock climbs gave me, the feeling of fun and freedom when paddleboarding with my dogs, being able to play a Mozart String Quartet, these are my motivators. That is life to me. I'm so grateful for everything I've been through, my journey, and what brought me to developing short daily routines I can use to help myself feel free from pain.

I thought it was complicated, but it's not. Otherwise, I would have helped myself when I was a music student, twenty plus years ago.

Eventually, I learned that simple techniques, including muscle movements or stretches, whether you call it yoga or something else, paired with acu-points from the ancient wisdom of Chinese Medicine that you can press on yourself, as well as intentional thought patterns could literally change my life.

I've seen too many people diagnosed and experience chronic back pain, where they thought "this is it, this is the end". They had a diagnosis and their body was in a certain state and they felt the only answer was surgery, medication or a life of misery.

Over the years of treating patients, I observed how much mental perspective plays a role in a person's recovery. In realizing this, I started giving patients homework, tools they could use at home between treatments. These include acu-points (acupressure) that they can apply to themselves or maybe some yoga ideas or stretches. In certain cases, we even talked about life, feelings, circumstances, and mindset of hope.

Through all of these observations, experiences, teachings, and discovery, I have concluded that back pain can be helped with a combination approach of sciences from several countries and centuries, sculpted into a short routine that can be used daily or as needed. The sciences I am referring to include Chinese Medicine, which is 8,000 years old from China, Yoga which dates back about 5,000 years from India and the field of Neuroscience whose literature includes ancient Egypt.

My ultimate goal is to inspire possibility.

I remember the mystical beautiful clear blue with light shining through, those sparkly blue spaces between the mountain crevasses, for inspiration, of change and possibility.

When you are standing on the edge and the only retreat is a forward retreat, look down into the crevasse, take a step back, start running forward, and then using all of your might and strength, leap! You will soon discover that you have crossed a great unknown divide and have successfully reached the other side.

Jenny Murphy

Jenny Klich Murphy

Creator of Back Pain Relief Formula, a program and method that was developed from personal experience and years of education and practice as a Physician of Oriental Medicine and Yoga Instructor, Jenny is a classical viola player and loves rock climbing. Mountaineering in several countries, she cultivated a perspective of reverence for the planet and people from varied backgrounds. Inspiring people to live fully and know their own personal strength and power in overcoming and transcending their physical pain through short routines including Chinese Medicine acu-points, simple yoga ideas and mind-set is what she loves to do.

After 12 years of treating patients with Chinese Medicine, primarily acupuncture, cupping, and herbs, Dr. Murphy identified a greater void for her patients that needed to be fulfilled. Observing patterns and answering the same questions time and again, Jenny saw that the missing link was to empower her patients to know more about how to specifically use natural medicine at home. Teaching step-by-step, personalized and do-able actions to take care of oneself, how to apply the methods of Chinese Medicine at home, and how to prevent body pain and health problems is her focus.

It was playing classical music professionally that created severe back and neck pain for Jenny. After her Master's Degree in Viola Performance, she moved across the country to study with a teacher she had before that had addressed the physical approach to playing. Jenny re-associated physically with her viola through self-created exercises, including meditation, mind-set and connecting with the parasympathetic nervous system. Doctoral research of "Musician's Wellness, the Psycho-Physiology of Musicians" led her to finding a book by chance on Acupuncture. The language of the ancient natural medicine made sense to Jenny and she soon found great relief from pain through acupuncture treatments. This whole experience led her to go to a Chinese Medicine School.

Acknowledging that doing activities we enjoy can possibly lead to body pain, Jenny offers a solution that can take little time and means you don't have to stop doing what you love or change your life completely if you don't want to. Including short practices of mind-set, easy specific word choices in line with the area of science called neuroplasticity rounds out her method approach of acu-points and easy movements or stretches. It's the combination synergistic approach that Jenny has found to be the best remedy. There's no time to waste, living life fully now is her motto. Be well so you can go out and do the things you want to do.

To view Jenny's Game Changer interview, scan the QR code below or follow this link: https://youtu.be/cwNIUW0Srgk

Jenny Murphy

My Wake-Up Call

By Shevelle McPherson

I wasn't supposed to make it this far. I was supposed to be a high school dropout, living off public assistance, have more children out of wedlock before age 18, maybe have multiple "baby daddies" and those "baby daddies" would likely, at some point, go to jail, leaving my children fatherless.

But I am not a statistic...

I am the founder and CEO of McPherson Law where I provide legal services to clients in the area of criminal defense and business litigation. I am also the Founder and CEO of Shevelle McPherson LLC where I serve as International Business Growth and Legal Strategist helping entrepreneurs protect, position, and profit so they can grow profitable and legally protected businesses. In addition, I am the Host of Soarpreneurs Podcast, a Number 1 Best Selling Author, and an International Speaker.

The Journey that changed the game

I initially began my law school career in Michigan. During my second year of law school, due to personal health concerns at the time and the need to care for an ill relative, I transferred to Seton Hall Law School, located in my hometown of Newark, New Jersey. While attending Seton Hall, during my second year of law school, my older cousin, Mattie Brown, had taken ill. Mattie and I were very close. We even shared the same birthday. She was like a bonus grandmother. Mattie was everyone's caretaker. She was a tremendous help to me and my son, Lamar. Back when I was in college, I worked nights and Mattie was Lamar's caretaker. She would later become one of my greatest teachers.

Mattie was a frugal woman, but she had saved enough money to enjoy retirement and to start doing things that she loved but kept putting off, like traveling. After working for nearly 50 years and taking care of so many people, she retired and was ready to start living her life. Other than occasional trips to visit her sister in Chicago, she had never gone anywhere. This was all about to change (or so she thought). Mattie planned her first real vacation - a Caribbean cruise and was super excited to finally start living the retired lifestyle.

About a month before her cruise, Mattie became ill and was hospitalized. Her left leg was completely black and blue from the toe up to the mid-thigh as a result of poor circulation. Emergency surgery was scheduled, and her leg was amputated. Upon her release from the hospital, Mattie moved out of the senior community she had just recently relocated to and into my home with Lamar and me. I was now going to be the caretaker for two people.

THE JUGGLING ACT

During my senior year of law school, I was offered a job as an Assistant District Attorney (ADA) for the City of Philadelphia. After accepting the position, I relocated from New Jersey to Philadelphia with Lamar and Mattie, for whom I was now the sole caretaker. I started my career as an ADA in the Municipal Court Unit where I prosecuted minor offenses, traffic offenses, and conducted bench (non-jury) trials. I remained in the Municipal Court Unit for two years before getting promoted to the Juvenile Unit. It was difficult managing a huge caseload, appearing in court daily, and caring for Mattie and Lamar, who was now in high school.

My ADA position called for long hours. Many of my colleagues stayed to prepare their cases until 8 or 9 PM. I didn't have that luxury because I had a son and an elderly relative at home. I was always a private person, so not many of my colleagues, and probably none of my supervisors knew that I was caring for Mattie in addition to my son. Lamar was a star athlete on the high school football team and was in the local newspaper quite regularly, so he was no secret. Everyone pretty much knew about him. I was wearing several hats. I had career responsibilities, caretaker responsibilities, and parental responsibilities – there were many tough days. As an athlete, Lamar also had regular football games that I refused to miss.

Despite the juggling act, my career was going well. I had established great credibility with the judges and was highly respected in the legal community. However, my quality of life was poor. My workload was brutal and balancing the demands of my legal career as an ADA and caretaker was oftentimes draining. I loved being this highly respected Prosecutor, but I was not feeling so glamorous on the inside. I came home from work every day dragging my trial bag loaded with files to prepare.

Even though I couldn't stay late, the work still had to get done, so I brought it home with me quite often. I would come home every day, sit and talk with Mattie out in the sunroom, and then handle my parental responsibilities such as preparing dinner and reviewing homework. On football game days, I would squeeze that activity in too. At night, I would sit in bed prepping my cases for the next day.

On weekends I would often bring files to the hair salon and would prep cases while sitting under the hairdryer. I dragged case files practically everywhere I went because the work had to get done. And although I worked many nights and weekends prepping cases for court, I was on salary so there was no extra compensation for this type of prep work. Life was truly a balancing act, but the best part of the day was the time I spent after work sitting and talking with Mattie in the sunroom. Mattie had so much wisdom and insight and talking with her always put me in a good space.

THE WAKE-UP CALL

It was a Wednesday evening after work, and I was at a football game sitting in the bleachers waiting for the game to start. Bishop McDevitt High School v. Carol Dougherty High School. This was a highly anticipated game. The teams came out on the field and the game began. Lamar was the star running back at Bishop McDevitt. It was the 2nd quarter and Lamar had already made four touchdowns. He was all set to go for his fifth. The ball was thrown, it was passed to Lamar, and he dashed toward the endzone. Seemingly out of nowhere, came a huge defensive opponent that cut Lamar off causing him to twist his ankle and hit the ground. He ended up on the ground under a pile of players. I could see Lamar underneath the pile up unable to move. The referee dispersed the pile, but Lamar continued to lie on the ground motionless. I clamored down from the bleachers, ran onto the field only to be stopped by the head coach who said, "we don't want you to worry him. If you come on to the field, just comfort him. We think his leg is broken, but we want to keep him calm and we do not want to alarm him."

I walked over to Lamar and he said, "Mom I'm done for the season; I heard my leg pop." I didn't have the chance to alarm him. And it turns out, he was right. After being taken off the field on a stretcher and transported to the emergency room, we learned that Lamar had a fractured left fibula. He was scheduled for surgery. The next day, I reported to work. I was now an ADA in the juvenile unit. I went into my supervisor's office and said, "Lamar was injured yesterday playing football. He has been scheduled for emergency surgery. I will need to take some time off."

His immediate response was, "How old is your son?" Lamar was a well-known football player, and everyone knew he was in high school, so I was baffled by the question. As I stared at him, he continued, "Isn't he in high school? He's not a baby – do you really have to be there?" I was simultaneously shocked and speechless and that is rare. Clearly our concerns conflicted. Lamar was my "why"! I had him when I was 15. The world counted me out, but I was determined to succeed and provide him with a better life and better opportunities. He gave me such determination and was the reason I became an Attorney and not a statistic. After a "woo saaa" moment, I responded. "It doesn't matter how old he is, I will be by his side before and after his surgery, so I suggest you find coverage." I walked out of that office forever changed. I was livid.

THE EPIPHANY

I came home and immediately stormed into the sunroom. The sunroom was where Mattie hung out all day while I slaved away at the DA's office. The sunroom was so tranquil. It was like sitting in an enclosed backyard. It was always peaceful and serene, and this is where I had my daily conversations with Mattie after coming home from the DA's office wiped out and usually ready to vent. This was where she received an earful. She would hear the good, the bad, and the ugly parts of my day and my cases. I began telling Mattie about the conversation I had with my supervisor about Lamar and his surgery. She responded, "Shevelle, when are you going to start living your life?" I was taken aback. That was not the response I was expecting. I was just looking for her to calm me down as she usually did when I needed to vent.

"Huh?" I replied.

"Life is not a dress rehearsal – you only get one. Don't be like me. Don't get so caught up in your job and caring for everyone else that you forget to live *'your'* life," she said.

It was, in that moment, that a light bulb went off. I started to reflect on my life and all the decisions I had made regarding my career up to that point. I remembered how I promised myself as a teenage mom that I would beat those statistics and build a better life for Lamar. I recalled thinking about how hard I fought to beat those daunting statistics and become a lawyer. I recalled vowing to become successful, and I had. I was recruited to be a Prosecutor and served in, what most people consider a prestigious position.

I had served in that position for several years, but it seemed like the position was no longer serving me. I realized that at this point in my life, I wanted the freedom and autonomy to take on the cases I selected, to be able to attend football games and care for my family without question or checking to see if I had available sick time or coverage. I also wanted more financial freedom. Life as an Assistant District Attorney may have seemed prestigious, but it didn't pay much. I was making close to $50,000 a year with over $100,000.00 in student loans.

The only thing good about the pay was that it was consistent. I began to think that Mattie was right. I was an accomplished attorney with education and skills. I needed to create a lifestyle by design and begin to live life on my own terms while I was still young and healthy enough to enjoy it. After a little more reflection and conversation with Mattie, I decided to resign and open my own law firm.

THE PIVOT

I resigned from the DA's office and opened my own law firm. The very first case I was retained for in private practice was a homicide case for which I was paid $30,000. That was more than half my annual salary at the DA's office and that was to handle one matter, not 30 as I typically handed (sometimes more) while serving as an ADA. It soon became apparent that my decision to resign was a no brainer. My law firm quickly expanded to three locations and generated multiple six figures in income within the first year. I enjoyed the autonomy and financial freedom that I was creating. I also expanded my services beyond criminal law. I began to represent business clients as well.

After a few years of helping entrepreneurs resolve legal disputes with partners, resolve contract disputes, file bankruptcy, and avoid impending foreclosure resulting from failed businesses, I had another "aha" moment. I realized that most entrepreneurs were struggling to build profitable and legally protected businesses. I thought that if I could take a business from zero to multi-six figures in less than 12 months, I could help other entrepreneurs do the same. I realized that with my business and legal expertise, I could help entrepreneurs build profitable businesses while avoiding those legal pitfalls that they were currently consistently encountering and then retaining me to resolve. I decided to pivot and start a new business specifically for legal and business consulting and coaching. I founded and became CEO of Shevelle McPherson LLC where I have since coached and counseled numerous clients, helping them achieve income in the six figures and beyond range while legally safeguarding their income and assets.

I am so grateful for my journey. It has been a real game-changer for me. I've come to realize that every obstacle I encountered was a hidden opportunity. Every set back was a set-up for my next best move. The greatest satisfaction of it all is seeing this entrepreneurial journey come full circle as I am now paying it forward with my clients. I am living a life by design while using my wisdom and business experiences to help my clients create their life by design and build a business they love so they don't have to slave away at jobs they hate or no longer serves them. Being an entrepreneur can be very rewarding, and I love helping my clients put sound legal and business strategies in place so they can achieve their entrepreneurial goals. My business continues to expand, and I enjoy helping entrepreneurs across the globe start, scale, and soar so their business can also expand. I am enjoying the pivot.

YOUR NEXT BEST MOVE

In the words of Mattie, "Life is not a dress rehearsal." Are you stuck in a juggling act of trying to balance a job, career, lifestyle or business that isn't serving you? Is this your wakeup call? Is reading this causing you to have an epiphany, that it's time for you to pivot and begin building a business and/or lifestyle that you love? If so, there are no accidents or coincidences, it is your time to pivot. Do not wait until you retire, or a life, health or economic situation forces you to pivot; pivot on your own terms. Take some time to reflect on where you are in life and/or business and if you are not where you want to be, formulate your next best move and then take action. Do it scared, do it messy, do it imperfect, but like Nike says, "Just do it," so that you can ultimately pivot into a business and lifestyle that you love.

Shevelle McPherson

Shevelle McPherson

From teenage mom to a successful top-rated trial attorney and entrepreneur, Shevelle is a true Powerhouse. She began her career as a Prosecutor, Assistant District Attorney (ADA) for the City of Philadelphia. After serving as an ADA for several years, Shevelle moved on to form McPherson Law, a law firm specializing in Civil Litigation, Criminal Defense and Business Law.

Shevelle has been recognized as a Top 100 National Trial Lawyer, a Rising Star Super Lawyer and a Lawyer of Distinction. Shevelle is also CEO & Founder of Shevelle McPherson LLC, a Business Coaching & Consulting Company that she grew to 6 figures, in less than twelve months, while working it as an initial side hustle.

Shevelle currently serves as an International Business Growth and Legal Strategist helping entrepreneurs across the globe start, grow and scale profitable legally protected businesses. Shevelle is also an Award-Winning International Speaker and has been recognized as VIP woman of the year by the National Association of Professional Women. Shevelle is the host of "Soarpreneurs", a Podcast for entrepreneurs ready to start, scale and SOAR in business. Shevelle is extremely passionate about helping entrepreneurs accelerate their income and build profitable businesses. Shevelle enjoys traveling for both business and pleasure. She also enjoys spending time with family and friends and she LOVES to just lay on the beach.

Connect with Shevelle:
Web: shevellemcpherson.com
Web: myprofitprotector.com
Instagram: @shevellemcpherson
Facebook: https://www.facebook.com/shevelle.mcphersonesq
LinkedIn: linkedin.com/in/shevellemcpherson
Twitter: @shevellemc
Podcast:
https://www.stitcher.com/podcast/shevelle-mcpherson/soarpreneurs-uninterrupted

Scan the QR Code below or click this link to view Shevelle's Interview:
https://youtu.be/-Qta5-gzIdM

Shevelle McPherson

Would You Like to Learn to Waltz?

By Denise Thomas

Have you ever thought about the impact one question could have on the lives of others?

Our 15th wedding anniversary was on the horizon and a friend suggested a wine tour in Napa Valley. Wow. That sounded wonderful! But what would our kids be doing while we were away?

We left them with Grandpa. Our daughter, Brandi, was 9 years old and our son, Sean, was age 4. Grandpa was about as happy as he could be taking care of those kids. His face was beaming when we said goodbye.

They played baseball in the vacant lot behind the house. He took them to the children's museum downtown and out for snowballs for a cold treat on a hot summer evening. Grandpa had been the one to give Brandi her first snowball when she was just 18 months old. Strawberry. Then, at one point, he ran out of ideas.

He was learning how to Ballroom Dance and was becoming fairly confident. So, he asked Brandi, 'Would you like to learn to Waltz?'

Brandi had watched him dance once before, so why not? Grandpa taught her a few basic steps and turns. She was a natural even though she was a good two feet shorter than he was. After moving a few pieces of furniture out of the way they moved gracefully across the carpeted living room floor. Brandi loved it.

A few months later Brandi asked Grandpa to dance with her in the homeschool talent show. We drove to Grandpa's house every week so they could practice and the two of them choreographed a lovely dance routine. They danced to the song, 'Sunrise, Sunset', from the musical Fiddler on the Roof. Brandi wore her Halloween costume: a blue and silver princess gown, and Grandpa wore a black suit. They were placed last in the talent show line up and they stole the show. No one had ever seen anything so sweet as a grandpa dancing with his granddaughter.

Within a week, word spread to the Ballroom Dance community and the two were asked to perform at a public event where the audience would be filled with Ballroom dancers. Grandpa was more than a little nervous and thought they needed help to ensure he looked good for his grand-daughter. They took several lessons from his dance instructor to prepare.

When the day came, Grandpa was visibly nervous, but they were ready. From the moment she stepped on the dance floor Brandi's confidence and grace made it seem as though she had been dancing the Waltz for years.

The following year they were asked to perform for National Ballroom Dance Week, a dance exhibition for the general public held at a local shopping mall. Brandi chose the Tango as their dance that year and again the two took lessons from a professional instructor to perfect the finer points of the dance. Brandi wore an asymmetrical black skirt with red roses over a black velvet leotard and I stitched a single rose from the skirt fabric onto Grandpa's black shirt. When Brandi turned, the red satin lining shown as the skirt twirled into a giant circle. This time they looked the part. And again, they were a hit.

By now Brandi was 10 years old and had fallen in love with Ballroom dance. She continued to take lessons, with Grandpa as her partner, learning more dances and every year they were asked to perform for National Ballroom Dance Week. I could only wonder, where would this love of Ballroom dance lead?

Then something unexpected happened the year Brandi turned 12 years old. A group of teens attended a dance at their high school not realizing this particular event was specifically for the adults. What they saw would change their lives.: Their science teacher and her husband were Ballroom dancing and these students wanted to dance like that! After talking with their teacher, they formed an after-school Ballroom Dance Club. All they needed was an instructor.

They contacted the Ballroom Dance organization and found an intructor from the next town. Brandi and Grandpa volunteered to assist. They attended the club's first meeting, but by the time they arrived, every member had heard of this 12-year-old and her expertise in Ballroom

Dance. Although she didn't know it then, Brandi would be training three of her future dance partners.

Every week, Brandi and Grandpa taught dance for the high school club. There were football players, math geeks, cheerleaders, chess club members, honor society members, and everything in between. Ballroom dancing brought together the most unlikely partners, crossing all socioeconomic boundaries.

It took Brandi a year or so to realize something else was occurring. These students were learning more than Ballroom Dance. They were learning respect. Respect for each other, and respect for themselves. Unlike other forms of dance, in Ballroom dance the gentleman proposes a step, the lady then has a choice: to accept the step or not. He learns to lead, and the lady learns to follow. But in learning to follow she learns to trust him because he is watching and guiding her to a safe place. In learning to trust him, she learns to trust herself. She learns not to trust any man who is not guiding her to safety.

Then the students became more than just club members with a common interest. They became friends. Good friends. They celebrated each other's wins and were sympathetic to each other's losses. When Hurricane Katrina hit the area, one of the students lost their home, and the members raised funds and collected clothing to help. The club became a safe haven for many during those years. When everything else in their lives was turned upside down, The Club was their only constant. It was their 'normal'.

At age 14, Brandi chose a dance partner from the high school club and while training her partner also trained 12 of the club members for the South Central Regional Ballroom Dance Championship. She competed in several categories and won gold medals in the Youth Division and the bronze medal in the adult Pro-Am competition. Every year thereafter the students competed and won.

Seeing these teens in competition inspired other instructors to contact their local school districts to start ballroom dance programs in public elementary schools. This year alone more than 340 fifth-grade students from 17 schools across one school district competed in The 13th Annual Dance Challenge, an event just for the students in this district.

But sometimes things don't go quite as planned.

At age 16, Brandi had big plans for competition. She planned to compete in 3 categories each with a different dance partner: Smooth (Waltz, Tango, & Foxtrot), Rhythm (East Coast Swing, Cha-Cha, & Rumba), and Paso Doble. But six weeks before the Regional Championship, Brandi fell 12 feet from the platform of a zip line and landed on her pelvis. I'll never forget watching from 50 feet away, not being able to stop it, and hearing the 'thud". I could tell she was in a lot of pain, but she tried to put on a brave face. She couldn't get up from the ground without help. Friends who were with us were paramedics and an orthopedic nurse. The fall resulted in two compression fractures in her pelvis.

But for Brandi, the pain was the least of her worries. After receiving the bad news, she explained to her doctor about the competition in 6 weeks. Luckily, he was familiar with, and understood the body mechanics necessary for each dance. "Paso Doble is out. There's no way you'll be healed enough for the beating that dance requires." As her mom, I was glad he said this. We had witnessed a championship level dancer re-break her foot during a competition when she wasn't ready. The other dances would be a 'maybe'. Maybe, if Brandi doesn't move for three weeks and is in a wheelchair. Then have physical therapy for 3 weeks, and that's the only time she is out of the wheelchair or off of crutches. He was adamant. No dance training. She literally drops her crutches to walk onto the dance floor to compete.

Was this even possible? I wasn't so sure. But Brandi was determined. She canceled her Paso Doble partner. But would the others be willing to not train with her for 6 weeks? The Rhythm partner had never competed before and was not confident. He gracefully bowed out. Her Smooth dance partner had competed the prior year and understood the ins and outs of competition and was willing to give it a try.

When it came time for Brandi to begin physical therapy, the office placed her therapist who was a former ballet dancer. Brandi was worried this therapist might not prepare her properly because although ballet is strenuous, Ballroom dance and ballet are completely different when it comes to body mechanics, and she didn't have time for misunderstandings. Brandi asked to be placed with a therapist who works with professional athletes.

A week before she began therapy, I stopped by the office to drop off a video showing Brandi in competition, so the therapist would see the motions that were the goal. It was extremely helpful, and he formulated a therapy plan. He explained to Brandi that the difference between post-injury physical therapy for everyone else, and a professional athlete who needs to be on the field next week, is the level of pain they are willing to go through. She had three weeks.

During these three weeks, Brandi's Smooth dance partner met us at a dance studio, and although Brandi couldn't dance with him, she coached him from her wheelchair while I stood in as his dance partner. There was a lot to cover with the three dances, Waltz, Tango, and Fox Trot. We worked as long as Brandi could handle sitting in the wheelchair. After a while, she would become uncomfortable and we'd have to call it a night and go home.

The day of competition drew near, and Brandi realized she would have to do her therapy stretches before 'dropping the crutches' to enter the dance floor. She made a plan for timing her costume change and stretching just before she would be called to the dance floor.

Wearing her competition gown, Brandi entered the Grand Ballroom on crutches and was greeted by several friends and well-wishers, and more than a few odd glances. It's not uncommon to see dancers with wrist, ankle, or knee braces and the occasional cast. It's a brutal sport. But this was probably the first time they'd seen a competitor on crutches.

As the other dancers lined up in numerical order, Brandi sat nearby on the sidelines. Her partner entered the dance floor and Brandi stood, handed her crutches to me and walked onto the floor next to him. The competition began with the Waltz. Ninety seconds. The Tango. Ninety seconds. Then Fox Trot. Ninety seconds. Their technique was flawless on all three. When awards were presented, Brandi and her partner won the Gold Medal and the entire crowd gave a standing ovation. By then everyone knew her story. Everyone was pulling for them. Later, when Brandi returned to her hotel room, she broke down sobbing, "I shouldn't even be here." She was overwhelmed with what, by the grace of God, she had accomplished.

Brandi and her grandpa continued to teach the after-school Ballroom Dance Club throughout Brandi's high school years. As the students graduated high school and moved on to college, they started Ballroom Dance clubs on their college campuses. When Brandi began college, she walked into an already successful Ballroom Dance club that was begun three years earlier by one of the high school students she had taught. She quickly became president and choreographer. And again, without realizing it, Brandi was training her dance partners. One would become her husband.

Have you ever thought about the impact of one question? One thought? One deed? One action? At the age of 9, that one question, "Would you like to learn to Waltz", would change the lives of thousands of young people over the next nineteen years. Some call it 'The Ripple Effect'. I call it, sharing what you love.

"Would you like to learn to Waltz?"

Brandi continues to teach Ballroom Dance and she and her husband have competed in and won numerous championships.

To view the video interview with Denise, scan the QR code below or click on this link: **https://youtu.be/4CT0ZN-HE84**

Denise Thomas

International best-selling author, inspiring speaker, and coach to parents of college-bound teens, Denise's mission is to inspire, educate, and equip parents who take an active role supporting their children to live a life of financial freedom.

Denise is a 20-year homeschool veteran having homeschooled her two children from Pre-k through high school. Both attended their first-choice college on 6 and 8 scholarships exceeding $100,000 and walking out of school with cash in hand. She and her husband have moved more than 15 times during their 34-year marriage, and spent 5 years full-time RV-ing across the US and traveling abroad after sending their youngest off to college. Denise currently resides in Florida.

Connect with Denise

Website: GetAheadOfTheClass.com
FaceBook: facebook.com/GetAheadOfTheClass/
Pinterest: pinterest.com/deniseldthomas
Instagram: @getaheadoftheclass

Denise Thomas

Make It A Great Day – The Choice is Yours – Choose Wisely

By Jackie Simmons

You're reading this book and I'm wondering: "Have you ever personally experienced a "game-changer" moment?"

Of course, you have, I mean, I'm assuming we've all had the "game changer," chapter-ending moments of graduating from school, moving away, leaving a job, losing a friend...

All but the last one, is usually seen as paired with chapter-starting moments as well, new beginnings, of one sort or another.

Most chapter-ending/chapter-starting, "game-changer" moments are full of promise and some mixture of excitement and anxiety. Usually, for me, the anxiety comes first, and last month was no different...

Last month I had a "game changer" moment while listening to one 7-minute talk.

It was August 3rd, and my middle daughter Stephanie was welcomed to the stage to give a short 7-minute talk. I was her speaking coach at the event and giving her feedback was my role. I was absolutely thrilled as she started with a "startling statistic" and then my heart stopped beating.

"3,000 a day. That's the number of teen suicide attempts in America every day and the number goes up if you add tweens and young adults . . ."

The blood rushed out of my face as she continued . . .

"When I was 14 . . . "

Several thoughts exploded in my brain at the same time, and I started yelling at her in my mind: "Stop! We don't want anyone to know! NO! No one needs to know! Stop! Everyone in the room will know that I was such a miserable mom that you tried to kill yourself. Stop! This is being recorded on video, you have to stop . . ."

Somehow, I managed to stay silent, "calmly" listening, all my stress management skills in use . . .

Stephanie continued her talk with: "I still struggle with suicidal thoughts every day . . . "

I wanted to curl up on the floor and just start howling. Somehow, I'd managed to convince myself that those days of chronic uncertainty were behind us.

And just when I thought my heart was breaking, never to be repaired, Stephanie spoke the words that changed my life and started healing my heart . . .

". . . and yet I manage to find joy every day. Now I want to work with teens, tweens, and young adults to help them find joy every day, even if they struggle with suicidal thoughts."

Boom - you could've heard a pin drop when Stephanie was finished speaking.

Then I couldn't hear anything over the applause (and the blood rushing back to my head).

All of a sudden it stopped being about me, and started being about the teens who struggle and about the parents who live with the chronic uncertainty and anxiety, never quite knowing if life's ever going to be OK again.

At that moment, I chose to do whatever I could to assist Stephanie on her journey to help others. My community rallied, and on August 16th, an eBook of inspirational stories for teens published. Thanks to the efforts of all the very special people who wrote for the book, including

Stephanie and her older sister Katie, the eBook became an Amazon best-seller.

I believed that if the eBook earned a best-seller badge, we could attract funding to get the paperback book into the hands of teens for free. I thought we could get it done in time for the "holiday season," a.k.a.: the "highest-suicide-rates-of-the-year season."

I called to run the idea past my youngest daughter Jamie who has 3 boys.

"Jamie, remember the *Make It A Great Day* book project? Do you think if I sent a book to you that the boys will share the book with their friends and talk about the stories?"

There was a pause and Jamie asked: "Mom, you know why I get tattoos on my arms, right?"

???

"Mom, it's to hide the scars . . ."

Tears wet my face as I sat silent. Somehow, I'd managed to push away the memory that I didn't have a suicidal daughter, I had two.

Probably on one who met me ever guessed. I never was much on sharing, or as my momma might have said, "airing", as in: "we don't air our dirty laundry in public."

There's no laundry dirtier than this. Suicide is the blackest mark you can put on a family. The one unforgiveable sin in the religion of my child-hood. So, we'd never talked about it once the crises were over.

"Yes, mom, I think the boys will want to read and share."

"Cool! I expect the books to be ready before winter break. What else is up with you? . . ."

. . . and as the conversation wound down, I realized that while the boys might be willing to share the book and talk about the stories in it, Jamie wasn't ready to talk about her story yet, and honestly, neither was I.

The next day Jamie sent me a message: "I talked with the boys about my scars last night. I even spoke with a friend. Mom, it's the first time I'm actually telling someone about my dark times," and then a shocking statement: "Mom, I'd like to write a chapter for the next *Make It A Great Day* book, if that's OK with you."

I cried some more as I read her message. Over twenty years of silence — now broken. This meant that we could talk about what had been unspeakable and I felt free.

For the first time, it felt OK to think about my story and the impact being the mom of suicidal children had had on my life.

My story is about: "How the years of silence cost me opportunities. How the thought of being 'found out' had kept me away from standing on larger stages or marketing my courses or books beyond word of mouth and networking."

The lightbulb went on and I realized the full impact of my beliefs my daughters' suicide attempts had had on my business, my willingness to let people get close to me, my life.

"Holy Crap!"

Talking about this amazing revelation that evening with the members of my mastermind led to unexpected challenges.

A member of the mastermind pushed me for details.

She asked: "So, what are you going to do with this book?"

"Get it in the hands of teens for free."

Then she said: "You know they won't read it."

I heard the challenge in her voice and spoke what was in my heart: "This book isn't about being read; this book is about being shared. It's about getting teens to talk about their friends who've died and their friends who've tried. It's about breaking the patterns and traditions of silence and shame around something that is truly only about loneliness and pain."

"So, how will you get the books to the teens?"

"Good Question. We're planning on partnering up to get it done. Yesterday, I spoke to the local school board and I'm being introduced to people at Girls, Inc., The Boys and Girls Clubs, and other civic groups that have teen programs. The goal is for Stephanie to give talks and help teens talk by sharing her story."

"How much will the books cost?"

"We're thinking $14.99 on Amazon."

"OK and how much will it cost to get one book in the hands of one teen?"

"Hmmm . . . based on my last book, about . . .."
She interrupted my math with: "OK, so I don't want to get involved in distributing books, but I want to sponsor **500** teens getting a copy of the paperback book for free."

Mentally I went: "Oh crap . . . the paperback isn't ready . . . the paperback isn't even on my schedule until November"

My brain raced: "Jackie, you don't have time to do this! You've got your summit coming up next month, you've got speaking gigs, you've got your online course coming up, you've got . . . "

My mouth said: "OMG! Thank you!" and in that moment I knew that my choice to do whatever it would take to support this project was a solid one. Though with my plate already full, honestly, I wasn't sure that the choice would prove to be a wise one.

I had no idea how getting the paperback book finished was going to happen. I hadn't reached out for any funding yet, I mean the eBook wasn't even 2 weeks old, and the eCover wasn't good enough or even the right size for a printed book, and where was I going to find the time and the focus? . . . and then . . .

An angel showed up in The Woman Entrepreneur Network. The angel was in the form of a graphic designer named Lily Erdy. Lily got behind the project and an amazing cover got created.

And then, another angel showed up with the patience of a saint. Nadine Vernon, one of the co-authors of the book, came to my house and sat with me for countless hours of formatting and then, over one very long weekend, the paperback book was assembled and submitted to Amazon. That was August 25th.

On August 26th, the Buy-One-Give-One Mission page went live. The hashtags were chosen, and another angel arrived . . .

This one was in the form of a podcaster named Erin Strayer. Erin's a busy lady, yet she had pushed herself to write a chapter for the book, because the day after we first spoke about the program, her son came home from school with the news that one of his friends had taken his own life.

Learning that September was National Suicide Awareness and Prevention Month, Erin called me with an idea: "Hey girlfriend, what do you think of getting the authors interviews on my show?"

"Are you kidding me? When's the next opening in your production schedule?"

"That's a challenge." She said. "I'm booked until . . . oh, wait. What if I do a special series on a different day, just for the authors?"

"OMG! Really?"

And in that one call, we set dates and times, and Erin generated booking links for the first-ever Author series of The Erin Strayer Show.* My interview was set for Friday, the 13th of September.

As my interview day approached, I realized that there would be no way to put the genie back in the bottle and that my "family secrets" would never be secret again. I knew that Erin would give this series of interviews even more of her amazing marketing attention than the incredible job of marketing that she always does for interviewees. I wondered: "Am I ready for this?"

The day before the interview with Erin, I was on a call with the publisher of my book *Your Path from Secret To Success*. She asked: "Jackie, we'd like to help you with the *Make It A Great Day Program*; what if we plan a full-out book launch for next month? Are you interested?"

"Thank you! I won't turn that down. I know what your book launches can do!"**

My daughters' stories were going to be told in an even bigger way, and mine was still safe. I hadn't been as brave as my daughters when it came to writing for the book. My stories for the book are full of fun and deal with "The Elephant In The Room" and "Shouldville," that dark, dank place you live when you tend to 'should' on yourself and others. Fun themes and not what Erin was going to be asking me about on my interview.

Sleep was unusually elusive, so I turned my thoughts to my on-camera wardrobe, and away from the topic . . .

When it came down to it, my choice to do whatever I could to support Stephanie's desire to help teens won out, and I lived into the mission and chose to "Make It A Great Day" with an honest interview, and the anxiety turned into excitement.

I stood up and spoke out in support of teens who struggle, and in solidarity with all parents living in uncertainty and loss. I chose to #StartTheConversation.

Now, it's your turn. What will you choose to do with the knowledge of the epidemic of teen suicide?

Will you bring the knowledge into your community and connect your civic groups and schools to the *Make It A Great Day* book program?

Will you sponsor a speaker to come into your kids' school or youth group?

Will you sponsor teens to get books for free off the website?

Will you get a book for yourself and share it with your family?

Will you be the one to #StartTheConversation?

We believe that If we can get teens talking, we can get them help.

Please think of three people to share the mission site with. We will only stem the tide of suicide as fast as we grow a network of people willing to talk about it. Your help is needed, the difference you could make is huge.

Please share the message and help #StemTheTideOfSuicide and always remember to #MakeItAGreatDay!

(Special Announcement just in – another podcast . . . *"Almost Naked Conversations"* is doing a 4-part series in November on the *Make It A Great Day* book program.)

The mission site:
www.MakeItAGreatDayBOOK.com

Our Hashtags:
#MakeItAGreatDay
#StartTheConversation
#StemTheTideOfSuicide

Our Supporters:
* The Erin Strayer Show
http://bit.ly/MIAGDAY-TheChoiceIsYours-JackieSimmons

** Spotlight Publishing
https://www.facebook.com/Spotlightonyourbusiness/

*** Almost Naked Conversations with Szebastion Onne
https://www.facebook.com/theancshow/

The Game Changer

Jackie Simmons

Removing the "Cloak of Invisibility" from her business skyrocketed Jackie Simmons from Secret to Success in just 7 months. BUT that's not what this story's about and it didn't start out that way, anyway.

For many years, it was like there was an elephant in the room of Jackie's business. The "elephant" sat on her phone making sales calls a chore and focus a dream. Seeking help, Jackie started gathering certifications, the way some people gather seashells.

No matter how many personal and professional gurus she studied with, Jackie kept making the same self-sabotaging decisions.

Saying "yes" to helping others and "no" to spending the time to actually grow and scale her own business kept Jackie in a never-ending loop of unstable income and overbooked calendar.

Permanently "taming" her inner elephant didn't come as a result of a single strategy, technique, or mentor. It came when she stopped seeing her business as broken and started to accept every aspect of her business and her life as "good enough", just the way it was.

"Good Enough To Sell" is the system that took Jackie's first book from concept to published in only 3 weeks and it allows her clients to go beyond what they thought was possible and earn as much in one month as they had the entire year before.

Audiences grin, giggle, and get it when Jackie guides them to tame their own inner elephants and walk their own paths from secret to success.

www.jackiesimmons.com

To view Jackie's interview for The Game Changer, scan the QR code below or follow this link: https://youtu.be/iqR3N-EC0sY

The Slow Simmer to Success

by Jen Du Plessis

It was much like any other day. Dad was drinking his evening six-pack of beer, and mom was yelling about the fact that he was drinking and questioning where he was all day, where he was spending money, or was he even making money. I reluctantly walked into the house, and as usual, it had become physical.

I grew up in a constant state of tension. My parents were always fighting, and I remember being terrified that things would get out of control; that I'd come home to find that someone would be hurt…or even worse. My father was often drunk, and my mother was verbally abusive. It was no wonder he drank or was it that she was verbally abusive *because* he drank? Whatever their reasons, today was the day I decided things had to change.

I ran out of the house to my grandparents' who lived next door and into their cornfields where I often played hide-and-seek for hours with my cousins or the kids across the street. Today, however, I was alone again, on my knees, praying to God that this wouldn't be the day I may hear a gunshot coming from the house!

I could feel the cold dirt on my knees and the hot sun on my head; while at the same time, smelling all of the vegetables that surrounded me. All I could do was put my fingers in my ears and hope that I wouldn't hear that shotgun go off. It was in that moment that I knew things had to change. I knew that life could not be like this for everyone and it wasn't going to be for me either.

To add fiery to fire, I was one of the 37 first cousins and the only one

who was without siblings. I had 18 aunts and uncles as well, and two of my uncles were like fathers to me. They took me everywhere with them – cleaning carpets, cleaning offices, cleaning their rental properties, working the family garden center and oriental trading store - after all, they had to, or I'd be home alone while Dad was off drinking and mom was working.

These two uncles were hustlers, with great work ethic (a trait I learned from them and am proud to possess). IN fact, most of my memories are of going to work with them. They also gave nicknames to nearly all the cousins, such as Dan the Man or Jean the Machine, and for me, they chose *Jenny who ain't got a Penny.*

One of them told me, "You know, Jenny, you're going to be just like your father. You're going to be an alcoholic. You're going to smoke. You're going to have a horrible marriage, and most likely you'll be poor too." So, I kept a penny in my shoe so that every time that they called me *Jenny, who ain't got a Penny,* I would grab the penny out of my shoe and say, "No Uncle, I DO have a penny." At first, I didn't understand what he truly meant, but when I did, it made me feel worthless and alone. This is when I began my quest for perfection.

Perfection because my uncles would see that I was attempting to be different than my parents. Perfection would prove to my parents that I could make something of myself and would make them feel proud of my accomplishments. Perfection so that maybe Dad wouldn't drink or Mom wouldn't yell.

I showed the hunger for perfection in many different ways throughout my life with having stellar grades, becoming a pre-med student, being the best in sports, playing Flute and Piccolo in the local symphony while I was in high school, becoming an avid speed reader, becoming the only student on the advisory board for the National Lung Association (to learn more about the effects of smoking since mom and dad both did, and I was experiencing second-hand smoke), becoming runner-up in the Miss TEEN Colorado pageant, being on a competitive rifle drill team, square dance team and soccer player in college, sorority, and on and on – for my entire adult career and life…until 12 years ago.

I thought that by becoming the best in anything or everything I did, people wouldn't judge me, look down on me, second-guess me, think I was like my parents and amount to nothing. If I could show all of them that I could be much more, life would be great, and I'd finally get an apology from my Uncle. There was only one (albeit big!) problem:

The Game Changer

All of this hard work for years and years, it turns out, was merely me striving to please everyone, and not myself.

Of course, I didn't realize this until several years ago when I discovered just how unfulfilled I was. Something was always missing – relationships were not truly close, I had gifted my way into the hearts of my children and grandchildren, my husband was really like a close friend, and the only thing that was working well was my mortgage practice which was always on fire. During this time in my life, I had many successes and failures, but none of them ever gave me the validation I was seeking. Dad never stopped drinking, the nightly fights continued, and I never felt truly close to my family. That was until the day it finally hit me.

As with most evenings in our household, my kids would say "Mom's cooking tonight, let's go out!" – which meant that I didn't focus enough time on grocery shopping let alone cooking a meal for my family. This particular evening at a restaurant when my phone rang, I took the call as I always did; after all, a client needed me, right? There I was outside the restaurant, walking back and forth on the concrete-car-parking-stopper pleasing and serving my client, when I looked into the restaurant through the window only to see my family laughing and creating memories--- *without me in them!* That was the trigger I needed to begin what is now my mission in life and business.

This second breakthrough really changed my life! As a result, for years now I've changed the way I work. I am present and in the moment with everyone. I've learned to do what is best, for me and not for everyone else. I'm fulfilled and seek ways to be fulfilled daily. It can be something as simple as listening to the sounds of nature in the early morning. Or just pausing to take in the beauty of our 21-acre farmette at the base of the Blue Ridge Mountains in beautiful Northern Virginia. Or just playing silly games on the floor with my grandkids. No longer do I need to prove to anyone except myself that I'm good enough---for anything in my life.

Perhaps like most people, but maybe like none, I didn't have one event in my life that changed everything for me; I had several along the way, creating the slow simmer to reach what I now call success. Life is full of challenges and I'm sure there are more to come. But what I know now is that I can work through all of them with the knowledge that whatever course of action I choose, the decision is going to be best for me and not to prove my worth or validate others.

In my typically driven fashion-- which hasn't diminished by the way-- I knew I needed to help others - maybe because of the business I was in which has some of the highest divorce rates and requires people to be available 24/7; or maybe because I simply wanted to help other people achieve their breakthroughs.

Either way, I knew that what I've learned in my life and the success that I've had in business couldn't be kept a secret any longer. The ability to recognize in others that same drive to be successful is a great intuition of mine. More importantly, is the skill to see how people are creating massive self-sabotage by not aligning their core values with their true passions – those that **they** fulfill daily – with their business lives. I help people discover how to first align their desired lifestyle (spiritual, family, health, finances, relationships and cultural experiences), and *then* create a business that fits into that lifestyle; rather than trying to squeeze their lifestyle into the chaos of their business.

So often we are focused on our successes (as I was too), that we neglect what is most important to our sanctity. A friend of mine once told me that "people spend their entire lives sacrificing their health to create wealth, and in their later years they then sacrifice their wealth to maintain their health." So true, don't you think? We chase the almighty dollar and later, if we have saved, use that same dollar to keep us alive. My father used to say that he "would rather wear out doing what he loves than rust out in a wheelchair or hospital bed." I reflect on these statements daily to keep my priorities in line.

I've learned a lot of lessons in my lifetime, and I feel compelled to pass this knowledge onto others so they can benefit. I'd like to share with you something I call the 5 core principles to master a lifestyle business to help prevent you from being overwhelmed, frustrated, disconnected and struggling to scale your business; and allow you to live the lifestyle you always dreamed of while maintaining a thriving business simultaneously – keeping in mind that a life filled with values can add value everywhere in your life.

These five principles consist of Clarity, Community, Communication

Credibility and Coaching.

Clarity is by far the most important aspect of any life or business. Knowing your Why alone isn't enough. Your Why simply establishes the destination you desire; but having the discipline to align your values with your intentions daily is what will carry you to your Why destination. Consider the establishment of boundaries in your life and live up to them. Equally important in business is the clarity of your branding and messaging. Are these in alignment with your values as well? Do your business and marketing plans allow you to own your business, or does your business own you, day in and day out?

Second is your Community. Having strong business or personal relationships is key – in life really. In Dan Buettner's book, *The Blue Zone Solution*, he found that one of the keys to living a long life is to surround yourself with a strong community. This can be your church, your close friends, a great neighborhood. Regardless of which community you spend time with, simply having these strong relationships and connections adds value to your lifestyle.

It's the same in business: consistent engagement with clients and business partners can dramatically reduce the amount of time you spend with random acts of marketing. In Russell H. Conwell's book, *Acres of Diamonds*, he encourages us "to seek opportunities to find true wealth right in your own backyard." So often we seek new leads and new relationships (as I had done) rather than being present with and nurturing to those we already have. Whether you are nurturing or neglecting them will have a significant impact for you.

Your Community is the lifeline to your success, so I encourage you to start digging into the treasures you already have. There is no time like the present.

Next is Communication. Have you ever had to call the doctor to ask about test results? Have you had to follow up with a business owner about a proposal? The list goes on and on. Look, if I have to take the time to call you for the status of anything, as your client or customer; you've just lost my trust, respect, and my business.

There is no excuse because there are several ways to communicate in today's world. Your role is to provide such a great client experience (not just "customer service"), that your clients are compelled to refer you, talk about you and engage with others on your behalf.

Customer service is what you do for people. Customer experience is how the person feels after having worked with you. Master this and you won't have to work a day in your life. This allows for the scalability you may be searching for. Establish the right turnkey systems to guarantee the experience is impeccable with each and every client. Your business will run more efficiently and the effect you have on your clients will be priceless.

Then there is Credibility. Who wants to work with an intern if you can talk to the Doctor? You have to be the absolute best in your field, period! Personal and professional growth is paramount in today's competitive marketplace. The speed at which things are changing is mindboggling. Carve time to improve you, first. Then you can help others. It's just like being on an airplane, take care of your mask first so you can help your neighbor. To become a Master influencer in your marketplace, be consistently visible, on your terms and with the same determination that allows you to maintain your lifestyle first and foremost.

If there are designations in your line of work, get them. Learn from your competition too. Each of you has unique skills and tactics, even if you offer something similar.

Lastly is Coaching. In telling my story please know that I didn't do all of this alone. I had, and still have, several coaches, mentors, and advisors. Each of us has blind spots and mentors can help us find and overcome them, especially when we are craving to scale our business. Accountability can be invaluable to keep our intentions and values on course to achieve our goals much faster than traveling alone.

Each of these principles, in and of themselves does not eliminate issues or solve all the problems; however, with proper thought, research, strategy, and execution, you will soon realize just how simple and fulfilling your life, relationships, health, wealth and spirituality can become.

Looking back on my childhood, I'm not disappointed by the struggles I was handed, nor for the slow simmer of time it took me to uncover what I desired in life and success. Instead, I'm thankful because it made me who I am today. I'm accomplished, confident, intentional, happy and fulfilled. I was able to change the trajectory of my life early enough to enjoy life on my terms, and now I can't wait to help and guide you on your journey *to turn up the heat* from your slow simmer so you can live the life you've always dreamed.

Jen Du Plessis

Jen Du Plessis

Jen Du Plessis is a Speaker, Author, Consultant, Coach, Podcast Host. She is the Founder of Jen Du Plessis, LLC, Kinetic Spark Consulting, Black Fox Investments, and Valor Home Solutions. She the author of *LAUNCH! How to Take your Business to New Heights*, and host of the #1 Podcast Mortgage Lending Mastery.

She studied Architectural Design & Construction Engineering at Colorado State University. With over 35 years of experience in leadership, sales and entrepreneurship Jen was named in the Top .0003% of Loan Originators in the US and is a self-proclaimed serial entrepreneur.

Today, she is a highly sought after national and international Speaker, Consultant and Coach. She shares with entrepreneurs and sales professionals, strategies to multiply their results while maintaining a commanding and prosperous lifestyle.

Jen has been featured in such publications as:
- The Wall Street Journal
- The Washington Post

Regular Contributor to:
- Mortgage Executive Magazine,
- Mortgage Women Magazine

Seen on:

- Good Morning America,
- Sirius/XM Radio,
- Federal News Radio, and
- Mortgage News Network

To view Jen's interview for The Game Changer, scan the QR code below or follow this link: https://youtu.be/W60gnYQuelQ

Jen Du Plessis

From Silent Child to Confident Communicator

By Marjorie Saulson

While most toddlers say their first words by the time they are two years old, I didn't start speaking until I was four. I wasn't mute. If I wanted something, I would point at it and grunt.

This is not something I remember. I would never have known about the early part of my life if my older sister hadn't happened to mention it during a conversation we were having a few years ago.

By then, both my parents were gone; but I can imagine how worried they must have been by the fact that their younger daughter was unable to talk.

When I finally did begin to speak, it was in full sentences. I'm guessing that I was waiting until I was fully proficient in the English language.

My mother criticized my sister a lot; so, my strategy became to keep my head down and watch what I said.

There's a message that girls get from society at large which I learned at a young age from my Aunt Irene: "Don't be too smart; the boys won't like it."

That message appears to be as true today as it was years ago when I first heard it.

Due to family dynamics and the culture of the times, I often found myself feeling as though I was not good enough, so I went out of my way to prove the opposite to be true.

I worked hard to get good grades in school.

I obeyed all the rules at home.

I graduated high school at the top of my class, earned a Bachelor of Arts

Degree with high honors, and a Master of Arts Degree in Audio-Visual Education from the University of Michigan. (Go blue!)

I became a teacher, teaching Russian and French in high school. After a year in New York, studying at Columbia University, I came home to teach French in elementary school, and then in junior high where I was also the head of the Foreign Language Department.

But none of this made me happy. In high school I had begun to suffer from depression; and by the time I hit college, it became a suicidal depression. I avoided getting near windows in tall buildings for fear I would jump out; and once I almost drove onto an expressway in front of a speeding 18-wheeler.

I had a hard time making and keeping friends; and while most of the other girls in that era got married out of high school or college, I was considered an old maid schoolteacher, who didn't manage to get married until I was almost 30.

Creeping out of that pit of despair became a journey of fits and starts, blind alleys, and serendipitous miracles.

I was 26 when my father died. Not long after that, my mother suggested that perhaps it would be a good idea for me to see a psychiatrist. To this day, I am amazed and grateful that she was able to see that I needed more help than she could give me herself. That's a tremendous admission for a parent to make.

In a better place emotionally due to that work, just before I turned 30 years old, I met and married my husband. He had been widowed two years earlier and was left with a newborn son and a two-year-old daughter.

So there I was an instant wife and mother to two children, ages two and four, barely able to keep my head above water.

In many ways, mornings were my biggest challenge. Bear in mind, I hadn't spoken to a soul in the morning since I started making my own breakfast in junior high (aka middle school); but now I had to cheerfully and patiently help two little children to wake up, wash, get dressed, have the breakfast I prepared, and get ready for the activities of the day.

No longer was I able to creep into the day slowly; instead it was an instant dive into connection and conversation. I did everything I could to make the mornings go more easily.

Once the children were attending school, lunches were packed, schoolbooks and supplies were then gathered, and everything needed for the school day was put by the door the night before. We would check the weather forecast and lay out the appropriate clothing so as not to have to think about those choices in a rush the next morning.

That's when I came up with one of my many mottoes: "Mother's liberation is when your youngest child goes to school for the full day and doesn't come home for lunch."

As we came together as a family and the children were both in school full time, there was no chance of going back to teaching. Due to a demographic population dip, working teachers were being pink-slipped left and right.

Because it has always been important to me to do work I feel is of value, I began to devote my time to various organizations in the Jewish community, doing interfaith work, and working in support of the Detroit Symphony Orchestra.

Instead of using my voice to help students speak another language, I was out there using my voice on behalf of worthy causes, doing fundraising to support their work.

I started out hating doing fundraising. It was so uncomfortable asking people for money. That's when I learned the crucial importance of having the right mindset.

Finally, a light bulb went off in my head and I realized that what I was doing was not really asking people for money. It certainly didn't go into my pocket. What I was doing was offering people an opportunity to do a good deed.

My job was to make that good deed sound as attractive as possible. Their job was to decide whether or not that particular good deed fit within their philanthropic interests and their budget.

Years later, I realized that this was exactly the right mindset for sharing the products and services I offered to people in my business. My job was to create high-quality products and services and to share their value as effectively as possible. Their job was to decide if what I offered was good fit for them or not.

My volunteer career included serving as president of a multitude of organizations, including my own synagogue Sisterhood, the Volunteer Council of the Detroit Symphony Orchestra, and the Association of Major Symphony Orchestra Volunteers; as chair of two Symphony Designer Showhouses, and as a Certified Adult Trainer and Consultant for Women's League for Conservative Judaism.

One of my favorite positions was being the editor of *Women's League Outlook*, a magazine then published quarterly by Women's League for Conservative Judaism. I loved being able to work with a talented and dedicated group of women and to use my writing, visual training, and organizational skills to create an award-winning publication.

Following in the footsteps of my mother's three older sisters, who were all active in the Suffragette movement, fighting for the right of women to vote, I became the flaming feminist of my synagogue, leading the 18-year process to achieve full egalitarian practice. Rest assured that I got plenty of practice dealing with criticism in the process.

Through the blessing of being able to serve all those years in volunteer capacities, I was able to make many close friends, gain all types of leadership skills, and receive numerous honors as a result of my years of service.

My years as a volunteer are the source of another one of my mottoes: "A professional volunteer is someone who gets aggravated for free."

Progress was much more challenging in my personal relationships. Even though I grew up with a critical mother, our family pretty much followed

The Game Changer

The Three Musketeers, *"one for all and all for one,"* approach of loving and supporting each other.

My naïve assumption about marriage was that things would operate pretty much the same way in my husband's family. While I had certainly run across mean people in other areas of my life, I always had faith that I would be able to get along well with all of my in-laws. That turned out not to be the case.

It was incredibly painful to be seated next to my hostess at a family holiday dinner and to have her say not one single word to me until practically everyone had left the table. Only then did she speak to me to tell me what a horrible person I was.

As I sat there totally stunned, I knew full well that her opinion was based on her willing belief in the lies about me that were told to her by another member of my husband's family.

It took years of my own personal work, plus some joint counseling with my husband before I could speak my truth in an honest and respectful manner to this woman, even knowing that her immediate response would probably be difficult to hear.

Fortunately, things have greatly improved with the passage of time, combined with my own personal growth and belief in my own value as a person. One of my favorite quotes along these lines is, "Your opinion of me is none of my business."

Along with my volunteer work, I had always flirted with the idea of going into business for myself. Flirt is probably the right word because I went down a number of rabbit holes before finding a path the truly sang to me.

First, I played around with several network marketing companies. I only chose ones whose products I really liked; but somehow doing the business didn't float my boat. Besides, at that point in my business career, I hated calling people on the phone to try to enroll them in the particular company of the hour.

Then I got caught up in the whole real estate world, going to numerous seminars on all types of real estate deals, from flipping houses, to owning apartments, to storage facilities, etc. I never invested in a thing, and finally realized that this was not something that truly resonated with me.

I finally found my true love by going through a side door. There was a course on Voice Acting in an adult education program at the high school where I used to teach. Since I enjoyed public speaking and had been taking singing lessons for decades, this sounded like a fun thing to do.

Getting trained as a voice actor was both valuable and fun; but I quickly realized that breaking into voice acting (doing commercials, audiobooks, cartoons, etc.) was not only as difficult as becoming a successful actor, but that there was no way to leverage the work.

However, I don't regret getting the training for a single minute, as it gave me the increased ability to assist people in enhancing their speaking with vocal variety so that they don't deliver their messages sounding like a robocall.

After years of struggle to come into the power of my own voice, it became clear to me that helping other people break out of the jail of their comfort zone so that they could share their gifts with the world is what I really wanted to do.

At the beginning of the path, I started out by calling myself a Public Speaking Coach, but I was never really happy with that title. That's because I believe that public speaking is not simply giving a speech, it's any time you talk to someone other than yourself.

I had started out feeling pretty comfortable giving speeches early on in my life; but it was a real struggle for me to feel confident in all the other important areas of building a business – networking and making sales calls, in particular, were a challenge.

Since then I've found a number of other people who also struggle in those areas; it has become very gratifying to be able to help them overcome the same challenges and frustrations that I have had to overcome.

As one of my mentors taught: "Your mess is your message."

Effectively communicating your value and the value of what you offer requires three essential elements:

> Authentic messages that resonate with your ideal audience
> Powerful presentations skills (both spoken and written) that engage the eager attention of your audience
> The courage to overcome your nerves and fear so that you can communicate with confidence in any situation

That is why I am so happy to have finally found a title that truly represents the fullness of what I can share with people. I am a Business Communication Coach.

I look back at myself at four, finally starting to speak after only communicating with grunts. It feels like a miracle that here I am today, having been named 2017 Top Speaking Coach of the Year, and 2018 Top Motivational Speaker of the Year by the International Association of Top Professionals.

Henry David Thoreau stated, "The mass of men lead lives of quiet desperation."

I believe that people are desperate because they stay quiet. They have an idea about something they would like to do, but never share it out of fear of being told that their idea is stupid, that they're crazy, and that their idea will never work.

People who do hospice work often report that, as people reach the end of their lives, they express more regret about what they didn't do rather than what they did do during their lifetime. So, they go to their graves with their dreams unrealized.

My mission is to inspire people to come into the full power of their voice; to give them the skills and courage to share their message, their ideas, and their gifts with the people out there in the world who are desperately waiting to hear from them.

The Jewish tradition teaches that we are God's partners in the repair of the world. At first glance, that's a very intimidating concept. Fortunately,

Rabbi Tarfon teaches that, "It is not our job to complete the task, nor are we free to desist from it."

Get clear on which small piece of the world you aspire to heal and give it the power of your voice, so that you can live a life of meaning and purpose by speaking your truth and repairing your piece of the world.

To view Marjorie's interview for The Game Changer, scan the QR Code below, or follow this link: https://youtu.be/D2iS8FMS_NI

The Game Changer

MARJORIE SAULSON
Business Communication Coach

Business Communication Coach Marjorie Saulson was named both *2017 Top Speaking Coach of the Year* and *2018 Top Motivational Speaker of the Year* by the International Association of Top Professionals,

Marjorie empowers reluctant speakers, entrepreneurs, experts, coaches and authors, to feel calm and confident in any speaking situation, whether they are speaking to one person or to a thousand.

A professionally trained singer and voice actor, she often uses music and a variety of voices to get her points across in a humorous and memorable way.

She has graced the stage and led workshops in a variety of cities in the United States and Canada.

Marjorie is one of fifty women (including Oprah Winfrey and Melinda Gates) who are contributing authors to the book, *America's Leading Ladies – Stories of Courage, Challenge, and Triumph.*

Her clients say that she *"offers a wealth of insights from a lifetime of passion and experience"* and that *"Marjorie's insight, coaching, and positive plans for action are an enlightening booster shot in the arm and psyche."*

Marjorie Saulson

We Wove the Magic...

By Natasha Todorovic-Cowan

It was June 2015, and that month will forever be emblazoned in my memory in sharp, crisp, hard black pen strokes and with soft pastel colors overlaid and intricately woven into one another simultaneously.

Chris Cowan, my husband, business partner, best friend, and the love of my life, and I were in Rimini in Italy that year. We delivered an amazing SPIRAL DYNAMICS® program to a wonderful and appreciative group of people by the Adriatic Sea. We could see it's azure blue from our hotel window.

Wherever we were in the world, when we were together, it felt like home. No matter what language people spoke, their customs, food, or attire, when I was with Chris, I knew I was home. While we had delivered literally hundreds of those programs, this one was memorable. It was one of those magical events where everything went far better than our expectations. Our clients loved their experience and we connected profoundly. Chris and I explored the town, bicycled, ate gelato and fantastic food, and enjoyed being together.

That was the year during which we had finally committed to taking more time to explore the many places we were fortunate enough to visit and to relish our lives. We had flown nearly two million miles around the globe consulting and working with people on five continents. We had saved up our miles to do just this. We felt after more than a decade of some particularly bizarre competitor-related harassment and bullying by work colleagues and competitors – so much so that I was eventually treated for PTSD - they had finally given up and backed off allowing us to finally relax.

We truly had a lifestyle business where we could be together 24/7 because that is what we both wanted - doing what we loved with one another. That trip found us hunting down the best cappuccino in Bologna near the Leaning Tower of Pisa. The plaza was under construction, but the hills of Tuscany rolled out endlessly before our eyes. We saw the great art and architecture birthed in the Renaissance in Florence while walking the markets. Chris would soon be helping me haul my shoes, bags, and scarves in overly stuffed suitcases back home.

For the first time in a long time, while in Florence, I explored a bit on my own. I took a train to the Prada outlet because Chris was a little under the weather. Taking pictures all the way on my iPad enabled us to pour over them together later so he could see the countryside, the homes, the graffiti, the people and the lives being lived. That is our business: meeting people being people and seeing their different worlds.

The different worlds brought back a dream that was prophetic. Most people have had a dream that left an indelible mark. I realized on that train that I was living a dream I had when I was seven years old, one that stayed with me. My mind returned to that dream. I was in the darkness of space and before me was a circular stairway that went up forever, and down forever. When I ventured to the side and looked down, the darkness went on endlessly. As I landed on a step, it was an entirely different world than the previous step. When I clambered onto the next step, I found another world waiting for me to explore.

Many, many years later, I picked up a book entitled, "Spiral Dynamics". I finished reading it in a weekend. Somewhere between the beginning and the middle, recognizing my home in it, I knew this was what I wanted my entire life to be dedicated to. Everything fell into an easy and natural alignment. I met Chris, the writer of the book, and we connected like we were meant to be friends forever.

He was working with a business partner who asked me to join the company. To seal the deal, the three of us met at a diner in Oklahoma on the way to a series of meetings. We discussed my role in the future of the company in the corner of an empty American style restaurant, the kind with the great big red, overstuffed vinyl seats that make your legs stick to them. Chris sat on one side of me and our partner on the other side around a corner table. All I could see was a vision of things that would be fun, exciting, where I could contribute to the work in a context that included people who understood my essence.

My quirky sense of slightly twisted humor doesn't appeal to everyone, but Chris found me funny. And I remember saying something I didn't know I would come to regret deeply. The notion was ridiculously funny to me. I said, "You know, it'd be so easy to turn this into a spiral stairway to higher consciousness. Then, all the new age people would love it." Chris laughed. I laughed. Our partner didn't.

It didn't take much time to realize something was off. Our partner was unpredictable, volatile, secretive, and things weren't making sense. One day, things were black, and the next day, what was previously labeled black, he called white. The changes in position and reality felt like whiplash. They were rapid and nonsensical. Things started getting really weird, which I didn't think was possible. For example, we'd signed the contract (I was an equity holding partner). The very next day he told some colleagues, "No, we don't have a contract. She's not part of the company." Wait. What?!?! I learned the term "gaslighting" many years later – the insidious straight-faced kind of lying that was said with such certainty that a person would question their own truth, perception, memory, and reality in the face of an alternative "untrue" reality.

One of my roles was to build marketing materials. Because he bragged about success with a significant project, I asked for the contacts and introductions so I could write up the case study for both marketing and educational purposes. He ghosted me. Years later, I learned that he had made it all up. In the meantime, other things happened that just weren't quite kosher. Eventually, watching the shenanigans, I said to Chris, "If we don't get away from this guy, we're going to get sued." We parted ways within months of me joining the company. Within a couple of years, he had a new business partner - a new age guru. He began promising a stairway to heaven to his tribe, which would have been entertaining had so many people not bought it hook, line, and sinker.

Our approach was rooted in decades of serious research. At the time, I was under the misguided impression that people, once facts became available, would adapt to the new reality. Chris and I spent five years compiling his mentor's book to make the research, and facts, known to the public. Our former partner had become an influencer in a cult-like spiritual group. They turned their wrath upon us. Why? They didn't want their cherished beliefs undermined by data. We slipped into a surreal situation where we found ourselves harassed, bullied, undermined, for almost 15 years. Despite efforts to correct the spread of misinformation and falsehoods, we found that gossip seemed to have more traction than the truth.

The facts are more widely accepted today about the impacts of stress and the toll it takes on the body. While I've often said that it is easier to destroy a person than it is to evoke the fullness of their potential, that was my lived experience. The constant harassment, the never-ending threats, the disinformation, and purposeful misinformation campaigns, watching the man I deeply loved aching, hurt, and saddened while we attempted to press on while taking the high road was difficult. Believing that people would eventually see through the masquerade, things started to break down. I was treated for PTSD. My adrenals and thyroid stopped working. In fact, there was a period where I couldn't even walk 2-3 blocks. My hair was falling out. The brain fog was terrible. My energy was depleted. I couldn't sleep and wounds would take weeks to heal.

At the time, we were working with a significant client. We were clear and open with my health issues. His "toughen up" stance had me working harder to deliver and get through the demands. Chris wouldn't have it. Partway through, and despite my efforts to make things work, in the gentlest and most diplomatic way possible, he fired the client. It was made more complicated because this client had also become a friend. The one stand Chris always took was one of no harm – no harm to others, no harm to nature, and no harm to the future. Despite the money, despite threats and harassment, despite pressures one way or the other, he never lost his values or the core of what he represented. While he was deeply saddened by the situation, he didn't want me sacrificing my health further knowing I would push myself until I broke.

Chris was the kind of person who gave you total freedom to be yourself without judgment. He fixed things before they broke anticipating their future condition based on current trajectory and pressures. He was the kind of person who would find a $20 bill on the sidewalk and look for the owner. If a branch of a plant was broken, he would plant it, and it would spring into life. He was kind, funny, a genius, and incredibly humble and self-effacing. He was generous and thoughtful.

In the first months of my joining the company, I noticed he would write something, ask for my input, then put my name on the article. When I protested because I didn't feel I contributed sufficiently, he said, "don't worry, you will." His naturally inclusive nature was how his business partner's name ended up on the book. Because he had no ego, he didn't care whether his name came second.

However, as an artist and creative, he did care when the very person he had extended his generosity to framed him as merely an "editor". After he had spent years writing, with little to no support and input, he discovered his words and ideas in a different book (the partner had been pumping him for analysis, material, and had been using Chris' work to write a book in secret with someone else), and he was so misrepresented in a translation fed to the publisher who was forced to pulp the inventory. Throughout history, the gentle and kind have done their good work in silence while others tore the credit from them then silenced them. This experience was no different.

I was aware that some people saw me as "Chris's sidekick". I was even uncharitably called, "Cowan's girlfriend," to demean my contributions, but he had incredible respect for my thinking, my research, and my work, as did most of our clients. Chris truly believed in equality and in me and my work which he supported wholeheartedly.

For several years, I spent time researching a few key problems and issues. We were given a body of work which we pulled together, compiled, edited, and researched, into Chris's mentor's book, *The Never-Ending Quest*, a treatise on the nature of human nature. When we were compiling it, a data problem made me crazy? We spent five years putting the pieces of a nearly 600-page tome together. There was a data set that it seemed as if nobody noticed. But as I looked at it, I knew it wasn't right. "Why does he report one data set here in one way and a different result for the same construct in another place?" It was driving me crazy. I spent roughly from about 2003, through every class we ever delivered, collecting over 600 to 800 sets of data around this one psychological dimension. I wanted to solve that discrepancy in the book before it came out. That was one of my personal research projects.

Another problem plagued me, which was an understanding of the American political parties; why war made sense, how certain values were espoused, and specific leaders were reviled and idealized. And, I was also researching what made teams cohere, conflict, perform and collaborate.

Chris supported my interests, offered input when I asked, and fully allowed me to explore my interests while we also worked with clients, travelled, and conducted our certification workshops around the world. Sometimes, despite a hundred successes, it is difficult to forget the single painful experience. Perhaps that is how we are wired. When we were in front of a room, and we were working with people, we typically pulled them into a space of love, sparking insight, and transformation. Most of the time, we were able to weave magic.

This one time, Chris and I were delivering a Spiral Dynamics® Certification training in South Africa. I was closing out a presentation on some research I had done. Presenting a few of the more interesting results of my three-year research project on American political values using our framework, I was trying to draw some parallels between their political situation and our own. A male attendee who was sitting at the back of the room asked Chris a question. Chris looked over to me, replying in part, then said, "Well, that was Natasha's research. So, Natasha, why don't you explain it?" It was his way of redirecting the man to the source of the information and research.

The man watched me as I explained things a little differently, taking Chris's lead. Initially, I assumed I needed to change my languaging or take a different angle. When I finished, he turned to Chris again, "Chris could you say something about x, y, z.?"

Chris replied firmly directing him back to me a second time, "That is Natasha's research. Natasha, why don't you explain x, y, z." The consultant was not hearing me. It became clear that it was not a misunderstanding. He seemed to just want Chris to answer. By round three, Chris was getting irritated with the unstated premise. Chris, sensing some misogyny, refused to fall into the trap. He tried to get him to understand that I was fully capable of responding and he needed to hear it from me. Although firm, he was always diplomatic and he tried to communicate through round four, "You need to listen to what she just said."

It was very clear to me that I was being dismissed with the underlying message, "You don't know what you're doing. You're just a woman. Go away. Let me speak to the authority in charge." Throughout, Chris was trying to communicate, "She might be with me. While we're doing this together, she's an authority in her own right. You need to address her, not me; and I won't be answering. Give her the respect she deserves."

We later found out that he was part of an all men's club with no women allowed. Chris stood for respectful treatment, acknowledging competence and humanness, and his support reassured me of my value and contribution. It was reminiscent of the dream, the worlds I was visiting, and the work we were devoting our lives to.

It took us five years to put the work together, which had once been termed, "The Existential Staircase" until the folly of the title became apparent. It was the manifestation of my dream decades earlier. Within a few short months, after we had released his mentor's book, our former business partner came at us with a frivolous lawsuit. It took three years, it cost multiple, six figures, and, while we prevailed, our health took a beating. It took a few years to recover and we finally thought the worst was behind us. We started to enjoy our lives, and things were coming together.

It was June 2015 and we had just returned from Italy. We were toying with a few ideas for my birthday as Chris was getting over the bug he'd picked up in Italy. The day before, he went for tests at the clinic. That year, for my birthday, I got the announcement that Chris was terminal. He was told to get his affairs in order. My brain just couldn't compute that reality. As was his character, he practically organized things putting me first. There was no drama, though he told me two things, the first was to avoid the cultists because "it will kill you the way it has killed me." The second was to "do something with this stuff."

A few weeks later, the day after our wedding anniversary, he died. It was so fast I just couldn't process the situation. Grief is an experience that words can only poorly describe. It was incomprehensible how I could still be alive, walking numbly, barely seeing people around me. How could the entire world have shifted so dramatically, and people were carrying on as if nothing happened? It was as if a cannonball had gone through me. I was a two-dimensional cardboard cutout with a giant hole framed by a head, two arms and two legs. That cutout just wanted to crumple up and disappear. I propelled my body from one location to another wishing every moment that either I could join him or tried to figure out a way to fix this situation, to bring him back.

Telling people took superhuman effort. I could manage one call per day. They took what little I had out of me. A person who had been in multiple courses with us said to me a week later, after I summoned all my energy and strength to tell our partners the news, "Well, you like yoga. Maybe you can be a yoga instructor."

That was baffling. How could she have been a part of our world, watched me in my element doing my work, training, consulting, supporting clients and our students, analyzing data results, and say something like that? I never thought of doing anything else. Like Chris had chosen me and I chose him, this work had chosen me, and I chose it. There was no question in my mind that I would continue. The only question was the form that it would take. So, losing Chris, for me was not only was losing my best friend, my soulmate, the person I thought I was going to spend the rest of my life with, but it was losing "us". And, it was losing my business partner while losing the system of which I was an interdependent part.

I had to rethink the way we were doing the certification training so it would work more effectively. I had to confront, very thoughtfully, the problems that we were facing with the insanity that the world of "higher consciousness" brought to this work. I had to confront the way we'd been teaching people the approach. The evidence was that it took more time, more support, and was much more difficult than we originally thought. Not only did I have to redesign the entire program, I had to redesign the offer, and I had to recreate myself.

Stress does take its toll on a person's body; that combination of your biology and your external environment. Half of it's what we come to the table with and the other half is what the world brings to you. And I think that played a major role in Chris getting sick and dying.

So that's the, "I don't think you can crash more than that."

Natasha Todorovic-Cowan

Natasha Todorovic-Cowan, MBA, is the CEO of National Values-Center Consulting and owner of Spiral Dynamics brand. Whether your challenges are resistance to change, cultures in conflict, strategic partnerships, dysfunctional teams, incongruent leadership or strategic implementation, Natasha's experience includes unraveling the people side of the organizational problems from C-suite to shop floor enabling leaders to make informed change choices.

Natasha comes from a country that no longer exists. She lived in three countries before she was 7 years young. Five years into her dream career in the garment industry, she watched it disappear overnight and had to recreate herself and her future. As a part of two acquisitions, she is no stranger to change. Her techniques for seamless handling of corporate change are rooted in 70 years of research and application in a variety of contexts such as not-for-profit, the mid-market, global fortune 500 organizations, and government agencies.

Natasha has had more than 25 years of experience applying her proprietary Spiral Dynamics cultural DNA survey, leadership assessments, and change readiness index to predict hurdles to change and what you need when leading through it. She has delivered over 100+ *Spiral Dynamics*® certification programs in 14+ countries and on 5 continents. That means she knows how to help you get results!

Corporate leaders, their teams, executive coaches and organizations around the world are able to more easily become change ready, reaching their KPIs, get promoted, and having their teams and clients firing on all cylinders. Natasha helps you get to the heart of what stands in the way of evolving and accomplishing organizational and professional outcomes.

To view Natasha's interview for the Game Changer, scan the QR Code below, or follow this link: https://youtu.be/0IKs1GbhixU

When Faced With Tragic Loss And Overwhelm There Is A Light At The End Of The Tunnel

By Inthirani Arul

Have you ever experienced tragic loss and overwhelm in your life?

One thing I believe to be certain in life is that if we live long enough, we will experience loss and overwhelm at some point in our life. When we experience the tragic loss or the feeling of overwhelm that washes over us like a wave, it feels like the odds are not in our favor. I am not sure if you have walked that path, but I certainly have. Sometimes it's the small things, sometimes it's the big things, but it is something that we all face.

I know that in my life there have been several of those moments where it was just complete tragic loss or complete overwhelm and yet somehow here I am. Let me share with you an experience. It was spring of the year 2003 and my mother was in palliative care moments before she was to pass. My father held the phone to her ear so I could hear her last breaths and tears rolled down my cheeks as I shared my gratitude with her. My mother was diabetic and suffered from mental health issues. She lost her eyesight progressively when I was 9 years old. As a young girl, I learned how to care for her because my father spent a lot of his time at work and I was the oldest daughter in the family.

Have you ever experienced a time in your life where you felt you had taken on a lot more than you could handle? I did, because I had to cook and clean, look after my baby sister and make sure my mother was safe. Because she was diabetic, many times she would take her food and throw it away, and if she didn't eat it would become a life-threatening medical emergency. I lived in constant uncertainty. It was living in these conditions that I learned to become more alert, aware, ready to take action and connect with my SoulPath.

During this difficult time of loss in my life, I was on maternity leave from work. My son was not even a year old. I felt a huge weight on my shoulders and was filled with grief. My mother was someone who taught me and nurtured me to be caring and compassionate. She taught me to be loyal and to be more alert and aware during the times when she would suffer from medical emergencies or wander away from home trying to find a cure for her eyesight or because of the voices she would hear in her head.

As I grieved the loss of my mother, I came to realize how precious human life is even though, for all those years, I feared losing her due to the many medical emergencies I experienced with her.

I was in my early thirties and was living through an arranged marriage and becoming a mother of a young toddler. My husband had recently invested in a restaurant where he worked full time.

Have you ever had a gut feeling that there was something not right and it was not a good feeling? That was how I was feeling one night when I was waiting for my husband to come home from working in his restaurant which was in a small town about eight hours away. The last time I had spoken to my husband was that morning. It was about 10 o'clock at night and it was much past the time I had expected him. I got worried and I called his cell phone, but it just rang. So, I waited, and he didn't call me back. I tried to phone him again and this time the message just went straight to his voicemail. I phoned again, and this time, I got the busy signal. I tried phoning yet again and now there was no signal. Now, I was getting really scared and started to pace the floor back and forth, back and forth, back and forth.

I got this gut feeling that there was something really wrong. I tried to call him again, and again, and again that entire night. I did not sleep that night and he never answered his phone.

Have you ever watched a scene in a movie and suddenly you feel like the movie has become reality in your own life? I found it so surreal because at 9 o'clock that following morning there was a knock at the door. Exhausted from not sleeping and worrying, I opened the door and there stood two police officers in full uniform. One of them said, "I am sorry ma'am. There was a horrific motor vehicle accident and your husband was killed instantly."

I just stood there with my mouth wide open, in total shock, tears rolling down my cheeks. The officer said that the road conditions were wet, and a vehicle was trying to overtake my husband's van on the highway. My husband lost control of the wheel and went into the opposite lane, head-on into a semi-truck that was coming towards him. He was killed instantly. The person that was driving the other vehicle that was trying to overtake him was not caught. They said they were going to do everything in their power in this lifetime to find that person who created the accident. They also left me a package with information about resources that I could use to get through this challenging time in my life.

I closed the door behind them. After they left, I started crying really hard. I was in terrible shock. Have you experienced a time where you asked yourself the following questions? How am I going to do this? How am I going to deal with this? Why is this happening?

My sister and my father were the first people I told about the accident and they told me that they were committed to being there for me. They made phone calls and they helped me get things accomplished because I was in no shape to speak. I could barely even eat. My stomach was so tight and tense. I was worried about my young son and his future.

I had all these thoughts going through me. How do I get through this? I have a restaurant now, how do I deal with this? I had all these thoughts going through my mind and I had no idea what I should do next. It was just so painfully overwhelming.

After the funeral, I had to go back to the restaurant and figure out how to take care of it because it was a fully-staffed restaurant. I called the landlord because he had shut the restaurant down when my husband died, and the staff couldn't even get in. The restaurant contract was in my husband's name and I had to get it into my name so that we could open it back up. Everything had to be changed over. I had to figure out the staffing and how that was going to work to get it up and running. Every small town has an organization called community ventures where they have mentors and resources who help mentor small businesses.

Community ventures introduced me to this incredible, selfless, generous, and caring human being named Dave who sacrificed his time and offered his expert knowledge. After many hours of communication, I invited Dave to come to take a look at the restaurant. He got there, looked around, and then he turned to me and said, "Is this your dream or your husband's dream?"

In that moment I realized that this was my husband's dream and it was not my dream. I did everything I could, and I sold that restaurant as quickly as possible. The only way I could sell it quickly was by selling it to the first offer I got which was from a person who was only able to pay a month by month payment. After a few payments, the person said they were unable to pay as they had declared bankruptcy. I realized sadly, that I had to walk away and there really was not much more I could do but take the loss and move forward with my life. All I could do was tap into my inner strength and trust my faith in the god of my understanding.

Somehow, I persevered through everything. I remember one other thing that Dave said to me. When I asked him how much I needed to pay him for his time and support, he responded by saying, "You don't owe me anything. Just help another person the way I helped you." I never forgot those words. He was like a human angel that came and then disappeared without a trace after sharing his words. To this day, I am reminded of the great humanitarians who do exist in this world.

As time passed, I dealt with each situation as it came along and pushed through it as hard. As hard as each one was, I knew there was a light at the end of the tunnel, and I kept looking at that light. I kept moving forward and having faith that whatever happened was meant to be.

As time progressed, and after making all those challenging and painful decisions each day, and as I persevered through every problem that was brought to my attention, I came to a deep self-realization. I returned to the same type of work I was doing prior to the birth of my son in the health care field with adults with special needs.

I will never forget how supported I felt by the staff and special needs men whom I had cared for prior to my husband's passing. Many of them had come to the funeral service. I was so fortunate that the human relations director who also came to my husband's funeral reinstated me under humanitarian reasons. At that time the organization had never done so for anyone before. I was humbled and filled with overflowing gratitude and my life was never the same again! It fills my heart fully and I will never forget those who were my well-wishers and sacrificed and gave so selflessly with their hearts to help another person.

As I was going through this experience, I was dealing with my son's needs. He was diagnosed as someone with unique abilities very early on. A day after he was born, while in the hospital, two research students approached me from the University of British Columbia and asked if I would give my permission for my son to participate in an experiment. They wanted to put a soother in his mouth so that my son would suck to certain sounds in a study for speech perception. After the testing, they informed me that he performed above the norm in speech perception.

I did everything I could to raise someone who was well rounded. I nurtured him to grow through sports and music. He grew up in a stable family with a grandfather he adored who was a great male role model, and by sending him to a school that would challenge him and his abilities. Through this process, I discovered that in order to raise someone who is a leader and who was well rounded, I needed to also become a leader and work on improving and empowering myself.

Have you ever had a voice keep saying to you that you have to do something more with your life? I had this deep inner feeling and voice that was like a calling me. It was like there was something more and bigger I had to do but did not know what it was. I felt this desire and I was inspired and motivated to read more books, take courses and training, and learn from great leaders who are making changes on this planet.

I started seeking more, and I spent countless hours reading and listening to audiobooks and taking courses. I was led to meet leaders who I later came to discover had a spiritual aspect to them and I was on a personal growth journey. As time progressed, I was destined to meet the divine presence of Guruji Mahendra Trivedi who is the highest form of consciousness on the face of this planet today. He is the founder of the Trivedi Effect.

Through the grace of God and divine care, I have successfully raised my son. He is now 17 years old, is a senior in high school, and a beautiful soul. Today I am the CEO of a company called SoulPath Inc. where I help empower people to live their most authentic life. I am a Scientifically Validated Trivedi Life Force Energy Healer and have participated in three science experiments. The results are published in Peer-Reviewed Science Journals and my abilities are being studied by universities around the world. I am the author of two books, *The Self Esteem Survival Guide - the River Within Me* and *SoulPath: The Journey of a Heart-Centered Leader*. I am an inspirational speaker, a mother, and I couldn't be happier.

Just know that when you seek within and connect with your highest self, the god of your understanding, you can find the faith within yourself and push through any obstacle that comes your way.

Regardless of how challenging, how difficult, how painful it is to take one step at a time, find gratitude, look for the learnings, and continuously work on and improve your character. You will get to the other side, guaranteed. You will find that once you have overcome the obstacles, there are gifts you will receive from every experience you have gone through.

To view Inthirani's Game Changer video interview, scan the QR Code below or click on this link: https://youtu.be/7eq2P25XXr8

The Game Changer

Inthirani Arul

A Scientifically validated and evidence-based Life Force Energy Healer, Heart Centred Human Relations Leader, Inspirational Speaker, Author of 2 books, and Founder of SoulPath Inc.

Inthirani is gifted to empower single parents, health care professionals, teachers or those who are looking to grow and become authentic heart-centered leaders through her divinely gifted abilities so they can live their optimum life and step into their unique purpose engaging positive action in their lives and leaving an evolutionary legacy behind.

Inthirani has been a caregiver since age nine and has volunteered with the elderly and taken numerous courses and trainings throughout her lifetime. Through her own intuitive and inner guidance, self-assessment, and self-discovery, she was gifted the opportunity to participate in the Trivedi Healers Mastery program because of her fortunate affiliation with Guruji Mahendra Trivedi. As a result, Inthirani participated in three science experiments and is now a Scientifically Validated Life Force Energy Healer. Inthirani's abilities have been measured, validated, documented, and published in Scientific Peer-Reviewed Journals. She has also been a member of CEO SPACE and the Quantum Leap

Program through Peak Potentials Training. She is a graduate of the Counselor Training Institute, and an award-winning graduate of Dale Carnegie in Public Speaking and Human Relations Training receiving both The Crashing Through Award and The Highest Award for Achievement. She is also an Ambassador with the Women of Global Change. Inthirani's gift of engaging audiences and individuals is an experience of inspiration and personal expansion so they can journey within their SoulPath.

Because of Inthirani's passion for the elderly, special needs adults, and children she donates her time regularly to such causes.

Inthirani believes that within every person lives possibility and growth. It is through our own self-assessment, improving our character, continuous elevation of our consciousness, and reaching that place where we allow our spirit to be the leader that is when our life can flow in synchronicity. It is through our own growth when one empowers oneself, they can empower others around them, be it their family, their neighbors, their community and the world at large. Inthirani believes that by connecting to your SoulPath and achieving from that place of existence, you will leave a legacy with the service you were brought to this planet to gift to humanity.

To learn more about Inthirani and her science publications you can visit Inthirani.com or SoulPathinc.com

Reigniting My Confidence

By Ted Usatynski

I love coaching. It's a thrill to help people become more confident and see them transform into unstoppable leaders. I feel blessed to have the opportunity to do this professionally and earn a living from it. I can get up on big stages and talk about who I am and what I do with ease. But this wasn't always the case. In fact, there was a time when all I knew was self-doubt.

It all began with a phone call.

I was 15 years old, standing in my parent's house. I had just hung up from talking to my father. I was in shock. He told me that my sister needed to have emergency brain surgery. I'll never forget the sound of his voice cracking when he told me this. My Dad was a tough guy. He built houses for a living. If he was this upset, I knew my sister must be in serious trouble.

In a daze, I walked outside. I was thinking... *maybe I'm dreaming.... doesn't this only happen in the movies? Or to other families? How could this be happening?* My beloved sister, Joan, was four years older than me. She was my best friend when I was little. She had played with me, and loved me, and taught me, and watched over me... and now, she might die.

Over the next few days, I was thrust into a world I'd never imagined. Hospital Intensive Care Units. Doctors. Machines. My family's stunned faces. Joan survived brain surgery, but she hovered on the verge of life and death in intensive care day after day. I was standing over her bed, touching her, and just praying for God to let her live. My parents were horrified. Day after day, the prognosis looked worse and worse. She regained consciousness, but she could not move. She could not talk. She couldn't even breathe on her own.

Week after week, this dragged on and it slowly became apparent she would be a quadriplegic and need to be on a respirator for the rest of her life. The doctors only gave her one year to live. It took nearly a year of hospitalization and rehab before my parents could bring her home to care for her. Her life… my life… my family's life… would never be the same.

For me, the world was forever different. I was ripped open in ways that I don't understand. It was hard to talk to my buddies about it. Sixteen-year-old boys don't really want to talk much about sickness and tragedy. I began to think about larger questions than I ever had before. Life. Death. Spirituality. *Where is God? What is God? How can this happen?* I became entranced by movies and music where people were talking about serious, intense things. One day, at my aunt's house, I was listening to the radio and I heard a guy talking about Jim Morrison, the famous singer from the '60s. He was talking about how Morrison and his band, *The Doors*, were trying to create music that healed people, which helped them break through to new dimensions of consciousness. He described Morrison as a SHAMAN… a word I had never heard before. I was totally transfixed.

I became obsessed with music and learning all I could about shamanism. Eventually, that led to all sorts of new worlds… psychology… meditation… neurobiology… philosophy.

I didn't know it at the time, but some kind of healing process had begun.

And I think it was the music that first spoke to me. I was hearing, for the first time, an intensity, an emotional, instinctual, spiritual swirl of human energy that matched the intensity of pain that I was feeling from my sister's tragedy. For the first time, I didn't feel so alone, and there was a tiny intuition that I was going to make sense of the terror and the profound glimpse of the edge of life and death I had witnessed from Joan's horrible suffering.

This is how it is for so many of us. At some point in our lives, we hit a bottom. And then we find something or someone that inspires us. It's like some secret doorway in the universe somehow opens for us and we get shown a little light.

My secret doorway was the music. It spoke to my heart directly. It bypassed my thoughts and fears. It reached me at my instinctual core. I became fascinated with this experience. What is this ability of humans to heal? How do we grow, change, and develop? What force gives us the strength to crawl out of the deepest holes of hell and climb towards something better?

Something in me recognized this force, this instinct to survive and grow.

I slowly learned to trust this deep instinctual intelligence. All the while, I was inspired by my sister, the bravest person I've ever known. She managed to adapt. Somehow, she made it back to college and even earned a degree in computer programming. Joan was so heroic. Can you imagine going back to college—that time in your life when how you look and who your friends are mean everything—in a wheelchair? How she ever summoned the courage to do this, I'll never know.

One moment stands out in my mind. Joan wanted to go out to a shopping mall. This was in the early 1980s before there were a lot of wheelchair ramps and other building codes that allowed people with disabilities easy access to public buildings. But her heart was set on this. We drove out to the mall and finally found a parking place. There were escalators everywhere and stairs. But no elevators to bring us up to the second-floor mall shopping area. Joan was crushed. My heart was breaking because I couldn't bear how discouraged she was. I walked around the entire mall and finally found a service area and I found an old elevator hidden in the corner. We had hope!

We got in and realized it was a pretty old elevator and it was shaky. But it was only one story up. Slowly we ascended. The elevator rocked and jumped, and the doors opened. We could see the mall… but the old elevator somehow got jammed and left us about six inches short of the floor of the mall.

I looked at Joan and she said, "What are we going to do?" She knew that we couldn't make it. Here was the problem: My sister was in a fully electric wheelchair that weighed about 200 pounds. She weighed about 150, plus, she had a giant respirator machine that weighed another 50 pounds. The six-inch barrier might as well have been six feet.

We had come so far. For my sister, going to the mall would represent being normal in some way. She could be out among other people and just be a "regular person" at the mall.
She whispered…"It doesn't matter".

I knew it did. She was so dejected I could not bear it. I had to do something. Anything.

I looked around the area next to the elevator. It was a service area where they brought in cleaning equipment and machines. I searched high and low. Miraculously, I found two short strong pieces of wood that I hoped would serve as a ramp for Joan's wheelchair to get her out of the elevator and onto the floor of the mall. I put the wood in place and, using every ounce of strength I had, I dragged her wheelchair up the makeshift ramp. Somehow, we made it.

I'll never forget that feeling or the look on Joan's face as she started wheeling into the fancy shopping area. She had made it. For a brief period of time, she forgot about her tragic life and simply enjoyed the mall like everyone else.

The feeling this gave me opened up an entire world for me. It was the feeling of helping someone else achieve their dream. I was part of something bigger than myself. Sure, I felt pleasure and pride. But there was something else. I could feel my sister's joy—as if it were my own.

Sometimes I think she incarnated on this planet just to teach me this.

As the years went on, I also managed to get my undergraduate degree and stabilize my life. I did pretty well in business school and ended up getting a job in investment banking. I was so jazzed, like any 23-year-old with his first big job, working in New York City and Boston. After a few months, I had made enough money to buy a new suit. And not just any suit. An Armani. A top-shelf, custom-tailored Armani suit. With this suit, I would surely rise to the top and be the envy of my peers. Women would swoon when they saw me, and surely, I would be on my way to becoming a Master of the Universe.

I remember the first day I wore it. I took the long way to the office, walking block after block, strutting in my new suit. Then I went out for lunch, just walking around in my new Armani suit. I had earned this. I was THE MAN. But something was off. It wasn't producing the satisfaction I was hoping for. By the end of the day, I just went home and felt so incredibly sad. I took my suit off and just sat there. Then I realized something profound:

Yes, my expensive Armani suit was cool. I felt pride buying it, wearing it, and having an impressive job.

But it didn't feel as good as helping my sister out of the elevator and bringing joy to her life.

The next day, I walked into my boss's office and told him I was quitting. I returned to my love of psychology, spirituality, and human development. My "instinctual roots," you could say. I became a serious scholar and earned a graduate degree from Harvard where I grounded myself in the fundamentals of neuroscience, Tibetan Buddhism, and psychology. I was driven by an instinct to heal, to understand, and to somehow enter more deeply into the profound opening I had experienced from Joan's tragedy. Eventually, this led me to Tibet, where I could gaze into the eyes of these great mystics and practice in their temples for a while.

When I got back to the US, I continued to take the long hard steps to bring together these transcendent experiences with my flesh and blood body. My desire to help others drove me to get my degree in counseling psychology from Naropa University. I could see how my own healing path could also be of service to others. I began to study the treatment of trauma and to recognize how my own life had been shaped so profoundly by the overwhelming experiences I had had as a teenager. I learned the science behind my journey. I learned how the slow road of becoming more present, releasing the shock, and becoming more grounded—in relationship to myself and to others—is built neuron by neuron.

Slowly, I began to notice that I was maturing and dedicating myself to this integration of neuroscience, trauma healing and spirituality in ways that were really in service to others. I was in the process of beginning my career as a coach and working on my first book, called *Instinctual Intelligence.* I was ready to GO.

Then, very suddenly, in 2006 my life changed again:

Joan's health began to fail, 27 years after her original catastrophic surgery. Her passing was another rite of passage for me, coming full circle. I was able to stay present to the extreme intensity of the death space—and be present for my mother who was there with me as my sister took her last breath.

As we were recovering from this shock, my father died, and just a year or so after that my mother got cancer and passed away. I felt shocked and disoriented. My career was interrupted. I had to delay the launch of my book and my professional career. I was grieving the loss of my sister and helping my aging parents through their sickness and death. Needless to say, I wasn't able to put full effort and concentration into my work.

But something else was happening:

I was losing confidence... not only in myself, but I was also losing confidence in life itself. I mean, I felt so uncertain. I was unable to trust anything.

You see, after everything that happened, I was too shocked and disoriented to really pull myself together and I just wasn't able to muster the energy and focus I needed.

I'm sharing this because we all get into situations where we feel like we're off track. Life throws us in a different direction than where we wanted to go. We lose people we love. A relationship ends. A business venture fails. We begin to doubt ourselves and other people. It can really undermine the confidence you need to create a new career for yourself or to take what you are doing to another level.

So, I want to let you know that I get it. I know firsthand how hard it can be to step out and claim your place in the world, to put yourself out there as a leader in your field.

But this is where I was, in 2012.

I found myself in a place where I had to reignite my confidence. I had to find a way to get myself unstuck, and venture back out into the world.

I had to get myself out there on a bigger stage, be seen by more people, and I really needed more self-confidence in order to do this. This was at the time when my confidence was at its lowest. I really felt overwhelmed and intimidated by other people who seemed to be having great success and were full of self-confidence.

I remember getting on stage in June of 2012 like it was yesterday. It was one of the first public talks I did to promote my book. I had anticipated that the talk I was giving would only draw a few dozen people, but it turned out that over 250 people showed up. The event center was packed.

The talk I gave was okay, but by the second half, I was feeling shaky and overwhelmed. Being on stage had made me feel even more uncertain about myself. I never wanted to go through that again.

I had to re-dedicate myself and apply what I had learned directly to my own life. There were so many important things I had learned in my life and career about this process from so many years of study, travel, practice, and working with clients. All the training I had received on high-performance coaching, mindfulness, psychology, cognitive development, and nervous system re-activation was my lifeline.

Using everything I had learned, I was able to activate my confidence step by step, overcome the fear, the hesitation, that was holding me back. I was able to ignite my self-confidence. I realized if I could do it for myself, I could really help others.

Over the years, I've written several books, developed on-line training programs, and worked directly with thousands of people all over the world. I founded the Confident Leaders Academy, where I teach these principles through online courses and mentoring.

Every day, I am reminded of *why* I do this. Sure, I'm really proud of myself for having achieved so much. But I believe there is more to success than making money. I am absolutely certain, that when I am on my deathbed, that it is the *feeling of helping others achieve their dreams* that I will cherish the most. And to think... it began with that day long ago when I helped Joan feel more alive.

We all want to get free from whatever is holding us back. If I can help one person, every day, break free from self-doubt and achieve their dreams...

I'll be one happy dude.

To view Ted's Game Changer video interview, scan the QR Code below or click on this link: **https://youtu.be/Ssaq5oKvrG8**

The Game Changer

Ted Usatynski

Ted Usatynski MA is the author of *Instinctual Intelligence* and academic articles on psychology, the neurobiology of Tibetan Buddhism, and healing trauma as part of spiritual development. He is the founder of Confident Leaders Academy which provides personal and professional training through online education programs and workshops in the US, Europe, and Africa.

He holds graduate degrees from Harvard University with a concentration in Biophysical Anthropology and from Naropa University in Counseling Psychology. He has completed training from the Sensorimotor Psychotherapy Institute in the Treatment of Trauma.

His newest book, *Men: Myths, Lies, and Reality*, co-authored with internationally acclaimed men's group leader Dag Furuholmen, has just been published in Europe. Ted lives with his wife, Gabrielle, in Colorado.

Learn more about Ted at www.selfconfidencemastery.com.

Ted Usatynski

When Life Gives You Lemons...

By Deneene Collins

I stood out on the freshly manicured lawn of the family home I grew up in with a little red toy cash register on a table surrounded by the toys I no longer played with. That was my first business. I don't remember how old I was, but I remember having a plan to make money by using what I already had. I didn't even know what the word entrepreneur meant, but I was one. I owned my own store, and the kids in the neighborhood were my first customers but they would not be my last.

With the familiar summertime smell of fresh-cut grass hovering in the warm air like a butterfly over a Buddleia, I floated into my entrepreneurial calling. Somehow, I knew I would soon be making money like the neighborhood boys who got paid to mow lawns. I was the proud owner of a first-class second-hand store, and even though my cash register was a toy; the money in it was real.

Eventually, I expanded my childhood business empire to include a lemonade and Kool-Aid stand with the help of a silent partner which was my mom. I was able to feed my pet pig Penny with all the money I was making, and she got really fat. Penny was my piggybank and she was stuffed to capacity with much more than pennies. My store with walls of wind and a roof made from sunshine was a business that would spark something within me to be my own boss one day.

The whole timeline is still a little fuzzy for me, but I'm pretty sure the red toy cash register came after the real white hospital bed I called home for months. One day I was at home with my brothers and I started vomiting and defecating blood. When I asked my brothers, who were eight and thirteen years old at the time to come and look, they thought I was being gross. The moment my mom arrived home, she knew something was very wrong and rushed me to the hospital. Doctors surrounded my bed like a wall, and they gave me at least forty injections that day. I had something they had rarely seen in someone my age, and they told my parents I would probably die. I did die, but the doctors brought me back. As it turned out, I had something called Acute

Hemorrhagic Pancreatitis. In most cases, it is fatal due to the non-stop internal bleeding that causes its victims to bleed to death.

I was in the hospital for months, and I'm sure all the money in my little red cash register and piggy bank couldn't have fixed me or paid the medical bills. I remember being in intensive care, wearing oxygen masks, having tubes up my nose, and I remember my mom spending the night at the hospital with me every single night. At one point they stuck a tube up my nose with a camera attached to it to look at my insides. It was miserable beyond explanation. I was a little girl facing a huge obstacle. My parents wondered if I would live. Since I'm writing this, I guess you know the answer to that question.

I remember kind nurses and I remember cruel nurses. One very mean nurse whose name I never knew, told me if I didn't swallow the nasty liquid, they were giving me to see inside of me faster, she would get it injected into me with a shot. Who does that to a little child? I don't know who she was, but I will never forget her. It has been said that people might not remember what you say, but they will always remember how you made them feel. In this case, I remember both. I believe everything happens for a reason, and maybe I went through that so I would one day be able to be kind to those I would meet who would be hemorrhaging in life and in their business.

Back then I didn't realize death was a possibility, so I had no worries of possibly leaving this world. I just lived through it all. I remember people praying for me like my grandpa and the pastor of the church my family belonged to. The hospital I was in was called Rainbows Babies and Children's Hospital and call it a sign or not; the day I finally left the hospital to go home, there was a giant rainbow over the hospital stretching from end to end. I think it signified a rainbow promise for business success that would be over my life after suffering death-like business experiences known as failure.

While in the hospital I had a two near-death experiences l as a young child. Actually, they were two very real death experiences. When the doctors operated on me, they didn't know I had a condition where I wasn't able to wake up from anesthesia without an antidote. The doctors and nurses discovered my rare defect when I wouldn't wake up after surgery. They woke me up with special medicine, and after that traumatic experience, I went to live with my family in Canada during a work assignment my dad had with IBM. I was the little light-skinned black girl with reddish-brown orange-colored hair and freckles that all the French Canadians loved. At that point I was also the person that made the Death Angel find a new client. I didn't know it then, but I know now how your difference can be the point of your significance. Little did I know that I would one day stand on stages inspiring people with my story.

When I lived in Canada, I enjoyed going to the café with my brothers to order les frites (French fries). We made friends with the locals and we amazed them with our American culture and American Money which was worth way more than Canadian Money. I remember seeing my brother's US money at the café and saying, "look, he has a whole American dollar." Unbeknown to me, I would travel back to Canada 44 years later to learn how to make money with my purpose while changing lives.

During my time in Québec, there was a man named Pierre I vividly remember. Every time I saw him in the lobby of the high-rise we lived in, he would teach me French. Once my family went back to the States, it was time for me to go to kindergarten, but I was too young according to the school system's rules. I was four years old and wouldn't be turning the required age of five to enter kindergarten until October which was after the school year started. My mother took me for a test to see if I was ready to enter kindergarten in her motherly attempt to get me in. During the test I spoke French fresh out of French-Canadian Canada and my French lessons from Pierre. They were so impressed that they wanted to place me in the 1st grade, but I was only four years old so my mother insisted they put me in kindergarten so I wouldn't be with kids so much bigger than myself.

School was something I excelled in until my dad got an assignment in San Jose, CA a year later. In Ohio, I was learning the *Letter People* and in California they were already reading, and they were also counting in five different languages. I suffered from culture shock anxiety and starting peeing my pants, literally. I think I was just really afraid and unable to cope with the drastic change and pressure it presented. My mom tutored me at home for one night and I went from a reading group I was in all alone, to learning how to read overnight.

My teacher Mrs. Otani was a kind, beautiful, and extremely patient Japanese woman. I thrived, made new friends, discovered the beach, and eventually went back to Ohio with the memories of a challenging but amazing life experience. Did you know that you really can hear the ocean in a seashell? Okay, maybe it is just air flowing between your ear and the shell, but that makes it kind of like a dream. During our beach outings in sunny California, we collected seashells and clams, but most of all family fun was our oyster and happiness was our pearl. Home awaited us, but so did the treasures of these experiences in our future.

My dad was always getting new assignments with his company. I had just started high school when he was sent to Tucson, Arizona. It was only supposed to be a temporary assignment, but they offered him a permanent placement. When my parents told me, we were moving to Arizona, the picture in my mind was of us living in a hut next to a cactus with the mailman riding by on a donkey. I had no idea what the heck Tucson, Arizona was like and I was prepared to make a stand against being transported to the desert against my will. I told my mom that I would chain myself to my bed and she told me that was perfectly okay because my bed was going on the moving truck. Bummer!

I always knew I was different, but when I got to Tucson and started school, I realized how different I truly was. The kids hated me and made fun of me, but I refused to change because of their shallow perceptions. After a while, they accepted me for who I was, and I made friends. I won the Tucson NAACP ACT-SO competition in poetry two years in a row and instrumental music competition one year, which allowed me to compete nationally. I even won the title for Miss Black Teen Tucson and Miss Black Teen Arizona. It was then I first started public speaking and realized what I thought was a curse just might be a blessing.

I began to knock it out the box academically and even graduated from high school when I was only sixteen years old by skipping my senior year of high school. I received a full-ride academic scholarship to Prairie View A&M University and that is where I got a real education. I'm talking about the type of education you can't get from sitting in classes and learning from professors. I learned about life!

The Game Changer

At times I felt as though sorrow was my major and joy was my minor. What I actually studied was Psychology and Biology, but what I learned was the anatomy of emotions and the physiology of preconceived notions. The history of my life was being made at a historical Black university, and the future of my life was being built on the cornerstone of gray area walls. This is where I would one day paint colorful pictures of possible dreams for those colorblind to racial inhibitions with full sight for visionaries with hearts made of prisms.

During my time at Prairie View, I made friends, I made enemies, I was naive, and I got super smart. Some of the friends I made back then, I still have to this very day. So much has happened between then and now including but not limited to friend-crushing car crashes, hotwiring tractors followed by a full-fledged police chase, having a baby out of wedlock and finishing school in spite of that, and many other stories that would make any big-time Hollywood producer beg for the rights to make all of them into a movie. I could tell you more, but I would have to kill you. The stories of my college days and beyond go on for days and years with multiple smiles and many tears.

In the late 90's I went to work for a seminar company. That is when I knew I was meant to speak on stages. I watched and learned everything I could from them. I listened carefully to every speaker's presentation. I observed how they conducted their live events. I sold their packages and provided business consulting services to their clients. In addition to everything I did for them; I wanted the stage and it wanted me. I left the company in 1996.

Years later I started working for PG&E. Shortly after Y2K, the company decided to relocate, and I was laid off. The end of that story started with a new one. I had read an article about a man who was able to make $50,000 in one month. I called him and before I knew it, I was flying to San Francisco to meet with him. He had achieved his massive success by conducting seminars. After the meeting, I went home and organized an event where he would be the speaker and we would split the profits 50/50. This was my first joint venture before I even knew what a joint venture was.

I was a one-woman show. This meant I reserved the meeting space, created the radio commercials for the event, I took the calls, sent out the confirmation cards, and held the event. As it turned out, this man wasn't a very good speaker at all, but he had a lot of knowledge, so I paid close attention to him as he spoke. After that event, I decided to create my own event. I used the knowledge I received from working for the seminar company along with what I learned from the presentation of the speaker I hosted the event for, and I constructed a masterpiece. The pressure I faced to deliver greatness transformed me from an entrepreneurial lump of coal into a diamond of a businesswoman. Sometimes you have to get dirty before you are able to shine.

The first event I conducted completely on my own was amazing. I was the event organizer, the marketing specialist, and the seminar speaker. I was closing $10,000 in a two-hour event, and I was on top of the world. Unfortunately, my speaking business was tied to the travel industry and it was going exceptionally well until 911. On a New York morning in a New York minute, my business crumbled with all planes grounded as the entire travel industry shut down and came to a screeching halt.

With a heavy heart for the lives that were lost in the 9/11 tragedy and with a hung down head for a thriving business that had perished, I went back to Corporate America. She acted like a woman scorned as if I had cheated on her by having my own business. It wasn't that Corporate American didn't love me; I learned to love time freedom and business ownership so much, I fell out of love with the controlling misconception of false security. Business ownership and time freedom had stolen my heart away from the thief of business ownership dreams. We are repeatedly told the phrase, "It's business; it's not personal." For me, this wasn't just a business thing; it was extremely personal. There is nothing more personal than your destiny. Once you begin to take your purpose personal, you will get serious about your business.

Flash Forward to 2008; I had lived a life of attempted business ventures all of which had failed! My daughter graduated from high school that year, and I graduated with my MBA. My mom and best friend in the world attended my graduation. Two months later in February of 2009 my mother, my biggest fan, and my rock in this world died. She had always encouraged me to publish and I never did. When she passed away, I felt like a liar, because I never did what I told her I would do.

The Game Changer

Immediately I published an online article titled, "Pancreatic Cancer - Living from Diagnosis to Death - The Diary of a Cancer Patient's Daughter."

I didn't think anyone would read the article, but 30,000 people read it. I put my phone number in the article, and I started receiving calls from all over the world from across the United States, the United Kingdom, and the West Indies. People were inspired and encouraged by my story and message. Lives were touched and changed with my words. I found my power in the pages I decided to publish for everyone to see and draw from. I became like water in a well for thirsty people who drank my words like the only thing that could quench their thirst.

I continued to publish poetry on social media when people started asking me for my book, but I didn't have one. After multiple requests for my book, I realized that the 200 poems I had posted online was a book, so I published it. At that time, one of my Facebook friends was a phenomenal artist living in India. He loved my writing and I loved his art. I asked him to send me all his art related to rain and nature which he did. Without ever meeting him or even speaking to him on the phone, I published a collection of his art with my poetic writings. The first book I published was *Abstract Poetry for Life* and it was good, but my next book would be absolutely transformational.

One day I was missing my mom so badly. I just wanted to talk to her again and I would have given anything just to hear her voice one more time, but I couldn't. That day, I decided to send her an email that simply said, "I love you and I miss you." Around two weeks later I received a response that said, "I love you and miss you too." I was paralyzed and dumbfounded by the response. I called my dad and asked him if he was still checking my mom's email. He said he wasn't which is when I firmly told him not to lie to me. Then he admitted he was but felt like I needed to hear the message he sent me from beyond my mother's grave.

That's when I started writing *Does Heaven Have a Post Office, Letters to my Dearly Departed Mother.* I opened the book up to other people to submit letters to their lost loved ones and it became a literary work of healing and release. People who had been in bondage to their mourning were finally set free. People I met through the online article I published when my mother first died even submitted their letters to the ones, they had lost they first contacted me about. This was more than a book; it was a collection of empathetic and healing expressions.

Fast-forward nine years; In the Spring of 2018, I traveled to La Jolla, California for a speaking conference and it was the first time I heard Iman Aghay speak. In 90 minutes, my life was changed forever. I didn't know who he was, but I knew I needed to know him. I knew in my heart and soul that he held a piece to the puzzle of my life that was missing. Within the next month or so I flew to Vancouver, British Columbia to attend his Ultimate Webinar Funnel bootcamp. Since then I've created Success Creation Academy, Inc., I've created my own online course, my radio interview broadcast invitations have quadrupled, I've been featured on numerous telesummits, I own the stage, and my future is becoming my present. I am currently training to become an international inspirational speaker and I am changing other people's lives in addition to my own. I'm changing the world!

I'm Dee Collins and aspiring and established entrepreneurs, authors, speakers, and coaches hire me to fast-track their success by uncovering incredible high income-earning opportunities in their own thriving purpose-centered business. They do this because unfortunately, most lack the proper information, direction and action desperately needed to do so. So I help them create, customize, and communicate their business offerings in highly impactful ways; showing them that the bottom line is: Every single day they do business, they must tap into the available resources that will allow them to magnify their message and maximize their business profits.

The Game Changer

Deneene A. Collins

Deneene A. Collins is the Founder of Success Creation Academy, Inc. and the CEO of Collins Consulting, LLC. She is an internet entrepreneur that publishes content with purpose. Deneene has published multiple books and she has helped and inspired others to become published authors as well. Her latest book, "Muscle Memory Millionaire" is changing the business landscape of success for many aspiring entrepreneurs. She is an International Amazon #1 Bestselling Author in the areas of Business Mentoring and Coaching, Educational Psychology, and Starting a Business.

Deneene holds a bachelor's degree in Psychology, a Master's in Business Administration with a focus in Online Business Strategies and a Master's in Graphic Information Technology all of which have equipped her with the knowledge and skills to uniquely position people for success. By graduating Summa Cum Laude from the Engineering College at ASU and receiving the Black and African Coalition Award for the Highest Graduate Student GPA with a cumulative 4.0 GPA, Dee has become a scholarly role model. After dropping out of school in undergrad to have a baby, she went back to school to get her bachelor's and then got two master's degrees back to back 16 years later. In the meantime, she learned valuable lessons from the school of hard knocks.

Dee loves to cook and displays this love for the culinary arts on her innovative live cooking show where people know her as DeeLicious. She is a media and marketing specialist who also enjoys traveling the world while sharing the brilliance and beauty of her travels with others. By many, she is considered a travel genius with her savvy methods for traveling to remarkable destinations at low cost or no cost.

This inspired her to create an amazing discount travel platform called MyTravelFreeLife.com. The program she created offers people travel freedom and dream vacation opportunities on a modest budget. After all, "the world should be our playground," is a statement this lady lives by. Dee is also working on a business platform that empowers entrepreneurs, speakers, and coaches to double and triple their sales and leads by offering high-value vacation incentives to their clients.

Additionally, Deneene (Dee) is an ordained minister. She doesn't tell many people this because she is spiritual and doesn't want to be branded as religious but wants everyone to know she is approachable and non-judgmental. Deneene, more commonly known as Dee is available for all types of ministry services across the US and around the world. She will even pray for you or counsel you if you need or want it.

Deneene Collins is an entrepreneur and businesswoman with an extraordinary heart for others. In the past she has hosted three major radio shows, "And God Said" with co-host Brenda Arnold-Scott on KWWJ in Houston, Texas, The Soul Food Radio Broadcast, and The Power Source Radio Broadcast on KGMS in Tucson, Arizona.

Writers, entrepreneurs, speakers, and coaches also hire her to help them self-publish prolifically and distribute globally. Deneene is an author, speaker, publisher, and international business mentor. Her business offerings are marked by abundant inventiveness that transforms creativity into productivity. Most of all, Deneene A. Collins is a forward-thinking entrepreneur that wants to help as many people as possible succeed!

Two things I didn't mention above in all the information I've given you are the greatest joys of my life, because I decided to save the best for last. My daughter Aveanie Chantél Collins-Stewart and my son Caleb Rashad Stewart have been the shining stars in my darkest of nights. They have loved me at my best and at my worst, and they are the very air that

I breathe. They are my "WHY", and the reason I work tirelessly to leave a legendary legacy. I would not be the queen I am without these two jewels that make my crown worthy of being worn. To my mom who now lives in heaven like the angel she has always been, you are still the sunrise for each new day and the strength in me that encourages me to tackle it. Daddy, you are my hero! My brothers, Brian and Bobby Collins along with countless other family members, mentors, and friends are a constant source of inspiration and support.

CONTACT AND BOOKING INFO FOR DENEENE:
(832) 630-9806   DEE@SUCCESSCREATIONACADEMY.COM

WEBSITE CONTACTS:
WWW.SUCCESSCREATIONACADEMY.COM
WWW.MYTRAVELFREELIFE.COM

CONNECT WITH ME ON FACEBOOK AT:
@DEECOLLINSOFFICIAL

FOLLOW ME ON INSTAGRAM AT:
@DENEENE_COLLINS

GO HERE TO DOWNLOAD YOUR FREE VISION BOARD CREATION TEMPLATE: PURPOSE.SUCCESSCREATIONACADEMY.COM

To view Deneene's Game Changer Video Interview, scan the QR Code below or follow this link: https://youtu.be/6YimyPOs87Y

Deneene Collins

"To be, or not to be"

By Jonathan Bengel

I believe many people may not know the significance of the quote above from William Shakespeare. For me, coming to understand what Shakespeare meant has required self-debasement, tears, and humiliation, that evolved into empowerment, growth, expression and–self.

Have you given anything to internalize this phrase? Let me tell you my story and think about what you are willing to do to discover what I have.

What if we said it a different way? "I am who I am. We are who we are. To deceive myself into thinking I can be anything different is **defamation**." To **believe** that we are who we are is simply a passive belief statement. When that identity translates into specific situations, we begin making an active choice. Choice is conscious: we control how we react to everyday situations, from name-calling and arguments to connection and even praise.

However, let me assure you, there are not many things we can choose to be.

I first met my best friend at the age of 10. It was 1990, and I recall always looking at my friend fondly. His short straight black hair, his almond smooth skin, and his jet-black eyes cast a spell over me. Because of his Native American roots, he taught me that our connection to Mother Earth runs deep like the rivers that flow through the rustic red mountains. We got into trouble together, played outdoors, and imagined we were flying to space from the top of the big oak tree that grew in front of our apartment complex. And of course, on occasion, he would let me play the latest gaming system of the '80s: his Nintendo. Ruben was my best friend. I just knew I liked him, but there were feelings unexplained feelings that ran deeper than Ruben being just my best friend. But before I could discover what those heart-surges were, our companionship slipped away like a ship sailing away from shore.

Jonathan Bengel

Fast forward to the Fall of 1992. I had not yet turned 12. Having asked my mother to call in "sick" for me, I turned on the T.V. "Ricki Lake" was just about to start, an American talk show of the '90s, which often competed with Oprah. The episode, "My Boyfriend Cheated on Me" started. I watched eagerly as if I was about to win a new gaming system of my very own. She walked to the side of the stage and waved her arms to the people backstage. From the minute I saw the first chiseled male face look towards his ex-boyfriend, I realized this was not your typical show: these were gay. As I saw the couples walk towards each other, it was as if someone had turned on the light. Instead of being dismayed by the discovery that Ricki Lake was interviewing gay couples, I loved it even more. I thought of how deeply I had resonated with the way they talked about their relationships. I thought of Ruben. And my heart squeezed. Ricki then said, "Let's meet those cheaters!" And out came other men! For a moment, I was excited! I had a word; a label to place on my feelings

I realized I was gay!

Now, most people would think, "How wonderful! You knew you were gay from a young age!" However, my joy was like a star in the distance. I could see it, and it was beautiful like it was supposed to be, but it was untouchable and painfully beyond my reach. In a moment that should have held complete freedom came nothing but self-imposed guilt. Self-imposed shame. In this moment, I judged myself. I looked inside myself and knew, from what I heard about other's like "me," that I was worthless, that I was a degenerate, that I had no place in society. Happiness and joy quickly dissipated from my heart, and instead, I was will filled with total fear.

You know where fear comes from? It comes from the unknown. From not knowing what will happen; or worse yet, it comes from us believing what we think might happen! I feared the worse. I feared what would happen to me if acted or if I told anyone that I was gay. I feared that my mother would stop loving me, I feared that my Tias and Tios would stop loving me. I feared the loss of my friends. I even feared for my own life. After all, I had read and been told that homosexuals were a sin. An abomination by God. Queer people were degenerates, and should, in the end, be stoned to death. The act of being gay, I had no association for the word; my feelings had not yet evolved to understand the attraction to my friend. They were just that; feelings. Undefined emotions.

You might be asking yourself, "but didn't you just write you realized you were gay?" Yes, you read correctly, but I know, you heard me say I found out I was gay and I didn't think I had a word to associate my feelings for my friend; but you see, hearing the word gay was just that; gay. No one really ever said what GAY meant; just that gay people were going to hell. The only real reference I had, as a child, was the passage from the bible, that my mother forced me to read.

Leviticus 18:22 says, "[Men] shall not lie with a male as one lies with a female; it is an abomination." Leviticus 20:13 says, "If there is a man who lies with a male as those who lie with a woman, both of them have committed a detestable act."

To a young boy, I certainly did not know what 'lay like' meant. In my mind, it was two people sleeping together just as I had lain with my friend when he would sleepover on the weekends.

As I sat there on the couch, mortified of my discover, I told myself I would never bring it up again. I would never talk about it again. Instead, I tried to repress it; to sink it deep into my mind; and so, the work to deny who I was, was set into action.

Many years later, while in High School, I heard of the one "out" gay boy. I was both excited and terrified to know someone like me (because it meant maybe finding a boyfriend,) but because it also meant HE would expose me for who I was! As luck would have it, he met me.

Our school orchestra concert had just ended. As we packed our instruments in the orchestra room, I saw him walk into the room. His blond hair glistening under the fluorescent lighting, his steel-blue eyes sparkling, and his milky white skin grabbed my attention. His eyes, like a missile tracker, made eye contact with mine. My stomach filled with fear, my hands started to sweat, and my heart pounded. I had nowhere to run, nowhere to hide. Like a lion who has spotted the zebra he wants to eat, Ricki locked onto me and made his way towards me. I tried to back away, but instead, my body pressed against the cold wall blocking me from escaping. Stopping me dead in my tracks.

"You look really cute," he said. Smiling and almost out of breath, I simply responded, "Thank you." Like a slow-motion picture, I saw him lean forward, his face becoming larger as it came closer to my eager lips, he landed the wettest, juiciest kiss ever! Having kissed a girl before I knew what to expect, but what I did not expect was a kiss that would forever change my life.

Having been kissed, my stomach filled with butterflies. My heart pounded, my body shook, and I fell limp into his embracing arms. I wanted more! To have more, though, I had to be his boyfriend, which we agreed to be. In being his boyfriend, it also meant the entire school would know my darkest secret.

The following day, Ricki went around school telling everyone he was dating this boy in school. Slowly, my peers figured out it was ME he was referring to. Now, you would think, what's wrong about that?

There wasn't anything terrible about dating Ricki, but if you consider being called "Queer," "Homo," "Faggot," and being spat and beat up exciting, then this was nothing like being excited. For me, it was like being stabbed at each and every turn. My "being" was on display for others to tear it down. To reduce me to nothing. It was pure torture day after day, month after month, year after year.

In my Junior year, I had enough. I decided that gay kids like me needed a safe place to hang out during lunch, to be free of the monsters. And so, I formed the first Gay, Lesbian, Bi, Transgender, and Straight alliance in the country and in our state of Arizona. I called it "spectrum alliance."

However, our club would be challenged by the school district; claiming that we were not a 'real' club. I, however, would challenge the district, debating that we were no different than the chess club, the football team, or any other club on campus. After weeks of long presentations and arguments, I got our district to back down and allow us to keep our club.

From there, our club-inspired many more LGBT Alliance organizations to form all over the country.

Being out was exciting; yet torturous. When I was selected to represent our school at Arizona Boys State; a political organization that teaches the top performing male students in schools, about politics I was nervous as hell because I knew I would be spending an entire week with other boys. Imagine the level of testosterone in one space!

As Saturday arrived, I caught the city bus and rode it to the pickup spot, 10 miles from our small apartment. There, under the hot Arizona sun, I saw an ocean of boys. All eager to get on the bus.

As I boarded the bus, I heard the taunting: "Faggot." "That's gay," "Shut up, you queer." Although they were not saying those words to me, I once again was afraid. I quickly went into the 'closet.' The "close" is a space where we go when we feel like our sexuality does not need to be 'seen.' It is also a place where we go to hide our true selves.

When we arrived at the university, we were ushered to our rooms. Sitting on the small dorm-room tables was a newspaper written by a few other members who were the "editors" of the paper. There, I saw before me opinion pieces written on the issue of homosexuality; being a homo was a sin, and that all homosexuals should not be allowed to run for office. Like a sharp knife cutting into my flesh, I took offense and quickly started to write my own counter opinions. Challenging their position on the matter. Back and forth, our ideas were shared. For and against. By now, the organization was in full anti-gay mod and few supporters who did not make themselves known.

Finally, on the last night of the evening, sitting in the remote back section of the auditorium, in a room of 600 boys, I listened to the speakers on stage. One after another, they spoke about homosexuality; it was a sin, it was wrong, and again, we had no right to be in politics. I had enough. Enough was enough.

I stood up and slowly walked down the long aisle. The stage growing larger and larger with each step. Up to the steps I climbed, the bright lights glaring down on me, and 600 pairs of eyes all looking at me.

I slowly grabbed the microphone and proclaimed, "Hi, my name is Jonathan Bengel, and I'm that faggot! I am that queer! I am that homo! I will not stand by and allow you all to just shame me and others like me. I will not just sit here in silence and allow you to put us down! I'm proud to be a homosexual!" Shaking like a leaf, I placed the microphone back, and as the gasp of air waved through the audience from the front to the back, I took my leave. As I stepped off stage, the moderators quickly moved to shut down the stage. Lights turned on, and the crowd went wild! "You got balls!" one kid yelled. "You are amazing!" another shouted! "I wish I had your courage!" another exclaimed.

It was at that moment that I realized that I am who I am. To be or not to be; that is the question! I decided from that moment on I would never hide who I was. I would never allow myself to be thrown into the closet again. I would stand in my power, I would reclaim it, and I would honor myself for how I am.

Many years would pass, and many more trials and tribulations would pull my sexuality into full question. I would be fired on many occasions for being openly gay, and I would find love and acceptance in so many more places and from so many more people.

Being openly gay now has brought me to a place where I can stand here proud of who I am, and it wasn't until I accepted who I was in complete status that I could work on growing my own multi-six figure companies, JB Financial, and Naked Tax Talk, and starting my own public Orchestra, where adults can feel safe to play in a judgment-free zone. Being openly gay allowed me to inspire my individual clients to make their companies go to the next level.

I learned that words are really empty. They have no real meaning behind

them. We chose to give them meaning. We decide how we will let them affect us. You see, once we take words that carry so much pain and hurt and embrace them as our own, to capture them and twist them into a positive, we cannot move forward in life. But once we own those words, those actions, and proclaim them as ours, nothing, not one single word or action can stop us from reaching our highest potential in life.

Now, I stand before you again, as that faggot, that queer, that gay man who made himself into something far more significant than those words could ever mean.

In closing, I ask you to step out of your own closet and embrace who you are in its fullest because here is what I know, once you do, there are no words or actions that can stop you from your fullest potential.

View Jonathan's Game Changer video interview, by clicking on the QR Code below or following this link: https://youtu.be/t8wr_02Y-vs

Jonathan Bengel

Jonathan Bengel

Jonathan Bengel is the founder of JB Financial LLC, Naked Tax Talk, and President and Co-Founder of the Phoenix Renaissance Orchestra. He is a Certified Tax Coach, Certified Tax Planner, IRS Enrolled Agent, and Fellow of National Tax Practice Institute. For the past 16 years as a Chief Tax Strategist, he created a multi-six figure company, created jobs, and saved millions of dollars in taxes for his clients year after year. He fundamentally believes that once you embrace who you are, no matter what, no words or actions can stop you from achieving your full potential.

Jonathan Bengel is the founder of JB Financial LLC, his first multi-six figure company. He tried to work in "corporate" America, but he was fired several times for being openly gay. "Enough is enough," was his mantra. So, he set out to embrace himself for who he is and fundamentally changed the way he saw the world around him and created a company that believes in a judge-free relationship.

Today, business owners hire him as their Chief Tax Strategist, because most lack the right tax strategies to legally outsmart the IRS, under deduct because most don't know what they can, and lack the right write-offs because they don't know. So, they continue to overpay and under deduct. He helps to unlock the mystery of taxation, uncovers legal loopholes, and reveals missed opportunities to create residual cash, year after year. The bottom line, his clients grow, prosper, and pay less to the IRS.

Most accountants do a good job of recording your history, but as a Certified Tax Planner and Certified Tax Coach, he helps to write your future.

As an IRS Enrolled Agent, he is licensed to represent you before the Internal Revenue Service, is borderless, and does his best to mitigate and eliminate tax problems. There is no shame to owing back taxes. There is joy in removing those taxes.

After many years of hearing the same concerns from clients, he created Naked Tax Talk; a show where tax experts, business owners, and the public come together and talk openly about their taxes, business issues, and personal development. Being who you are matters to him.

In 2018, having no one to play with, and not a master of the violin, he wanted to play with other adults. So, he formed the Phoenix Renaissance Orchestra, a place for 30 plus year-olds to reconnect with their string instruments in a judge-free zone. No auditions required. Again, you are who you are, a good player or a bad one. It does not matter, so long as you belong.

Connect with Jonathan

email: info@jbfinancialllc.com
letsgetnaked@nakedtaxtalk.com
Web: jbfinancialllc.com
nakedtaxtalk.com
Facebook: facebook.com/nakedtaxtalk

Jonathan Bengel

Forgiveness

By Sheridan Wickens-Fogg

I came into this world kicking and screaming, three months early, via c-section. My mother said I was odd-looking, very yellow, and reminded her of the baby out of the movie, "Rosemary's Baby."

My birth set the tone for my personality, always challenging the norm and doing things differently, sometimes the hard way.

I knew from a young age that I was different because I struggled with certain things and I would approach problems in a very different way than most people.

I was an emotional child and sensed the emotions of other people very easily as well. Sometimes I would share something I sensed about a person with them, things I couldn't possibly know. Later, in life, I learned that there was a term for that; Empath.

Learning was often hard for me, especially in school. As an adult, after the appropriate testing, I was diagnosed with ADD - Attention Deficit Disorder.

Being dyslexic and ambidextrous and going to a catholic elementary school seemed to point out these differences even more sharply. The nuns didn't allow me to write with my left hand and were very quick to give me a slap across the hand with the ruler.

My mum would always say that I was, "different" but not in a good way.

My mother had this look reserved for certain occasions that was designed to make you feel small and insignificant.

She would get frustrated with me and say, "Why can't you just be normal?" "Why can't you be like your brother and sisters?"

I tried very hard to be like them and do exactly as they did, but it seemed the more I tried, the more mistakes I made, and the more she would point them out.

All my sisters, my brother, and I were very close growing up. We used to go fishing, ride bikes, and we all loved to swim.

We were all very gifted in singing and playing instruments. and we were always singing, dancing or putting on little shows for just about anyone who would watch.

I remember those moments as being some of the most special times in my life with my siblings growing up. We took care of each other and had each other's back.

There were other times though that being in my family was terribly hard.

My father was diagnosed with depression and was bi-polar disorder. There were times when my mum would tell us to go play outside or to be quiet because our "noise" would get dad rattled and irritated. As a young child I had no concept of those medical conditions and just thought that dad needed a "time out" occasionally.

My parents would argue about the typical things in a marriage and the challenges of having children. Once, when I was about 14 years old, my mum and dad had been arguing. My dad was sitting on the corner of the bed and was just looking at the floor.

Mum was yelling at dad and asking him if he could tell his own daughter that he loved her. After a few minutes of silence, my mum left the room. Dad was still looking at the floor. I reached over to him and grabbed his hand and told him I loved him and that I knew that he loved me even if he couldn't say it.

That was when I knew that there was more to these medical conditions and that this was not normal behavior by any standards.

My mum wasn't without her fair share of problems. She grew up in wartime England in the 1940s where they had to ration food and grocery items. I remember her telling me how she was very excited as a child when she could get an orange at the local store because a shipment had made it through.

My mum was molested as a young child by her uncle or a friend of the family. She never got into the details, but this affected her in many ways regarding trust and relationships.

She had very low self-esteem and had both anorexia and bulimia. If that wasn't enough, my mum was diagnosed with Multiple Sclerosis shortly after I was born and told me she thought the pregnancy brought the disease on.

She shared with me that my sister and I were an "oops," an accident! We were raised Roman Catholic and the church didn't believe in birth control methods. After having me though, I guess my father and mother decided they weren't going to be quite so Catholic and mum went on birth control.

I have always looked up to my oldest sister Tracy and, as a child, I wanted to be her when I grew up. I love the grace and tenacity that she exhibits in the face of hardship or problem to solve. She is the type of person that people are drawn to and she makes people feel comfortable from the get-go. She also has the most wonderful laugh that when you hear it, you automatically smile.

Tracy didn't get to experience a normal childhood because she was taking care of us kids as our parents both worked.

I don't know if she ever resented us for it, but if she did, she never showed it. We all had chores in our house, from taking care of the animals, cleaning, laundry, and doing dishes. Tracy would make dinner and help us with our homework. She unknowingly filled the role of mother to us on numerous occasions.

I can't remember the exact moment when I knew that my mother suffered from anorexia and bulimia, but I remember Tracy telling me a story when she was about 12 years old. Mum came out of the bathroom after another self-induced episode of throwing up and collapsed on the floor. She was having a seizure.

Tracy had to call for help and take care of the rest of us kids while they took mum away in the ambulance.

There were many other instances like this, but I don't remember any of us saying anything to mum about it. We wouldn't dare.

Mum always had to look perfect; hair and make-up on, always wearing the most fashionable clothes. Your appearance, how you looked, what you drove and where you lived was everything to her. These were the traits that made you successful in her eyes.

Sheridan Wickens-Fogg

At sixteen, my sister and I worked part-time jobs after school at the local coffee bar. Little did I know that by working there, I would experience something that would be a defining moment in my life and would hold me hostage for many years to come.

I worked the late shift after school, and the coffee bar closed at 9:00 pm. The father of the owner offered to give me a ride home and I accepted.

On that ride home, I was molested by that man who was about fifty years my senior. I remember thinking two things.

1. What did I do to make this happen?

2. My mum is going to kill me!

I carried this around with me for the next couple of days and finally shared it with a friend from school. My friend did the right thing and told her mother who then contacted my mum.

I remember that day like it was yesterday. I was in my room doing my homework and mum had come home from work. I heard the front door slam, then she walked into my room and she said, "I heard something today and I really hope that this is not true because it will just kill your father. His reputation will be ruined." She then asked me if I was molested by the shop owners' father.

It took me no time to answer, I simply said, "no!"

You see, I was a daddy's girl, so my mother being the manipulative narcissist that she was, knew exactly what she needed to say to get the answer she wanted to hear.

We looked at each other, and at that moment, I was silently pleading with her to push me, to say something, ask me if I was telling the truth. But I realized that was not going to happen. Her look said, "this ends here," and I knew nothing more would be said or mentioned again about it.

That was one of the most painful experiences in my life, and to think that it would have brought shame or disgrace to my father or family in any way was more than I could bear. So, I had to remain silent.

In my immature mind, I was the reason it happened; there was something I did to make this man do this to me.

My mum's reaction, her thoughts, and feelings towards it, dictated how I should feel. Or so she thought; and so, it was.

If she had shown outrage towards this man for touching her daughter, held me and told me I had done nothing wrong, I would have believed that and been outraged too! I would not have felt the guilt, shame, and disgust I felt in that moment, and for a good portion of my life.

Many things changed for me in regard to my relationship with my mother. I began to realize that she would never be the mother that I needed her to be. I often wondered when or if my older siblings experienced a moment of clarity like this.

This was also the year that my mother took me to the doctors, said that I was suffering from depression, and promptly walked me out of the office with a prescription for Amitriptyline. This was back in the days when the doctors just listened to the parents and didn't really ask the child-patient anything. I don't think I stood on a scale for a weight check or had my blood pressure checked. The doctor never asked me how I was feeling. The truth was, I wasn't really feeling anything. I was just going through the motions. I still believed that my mum had my best interest at heart. That is what a mother does for her children, right?

When I was on the medication, I remember feeling numb like I was walking around in a daze. It felt like I was witnessing life going by like I was watching from the outside looking in. The medication made me very sleepy, and I felt even more isolated and "different."

As an adult, I look back on that time and see that I was clearly not depressed, I was a typical teenager, challenging authority, going through hormone changes, and admittingly acting out a bit towards my mum.

These events also affected my relationship with my father and my interaction with men. To this day, I still find it difficult to receive hugs from older gentlemen with greying hair and I have a deep mistrust of men in general.

It is interesting how our minds respond to trauma and stress as individuals.

I lived with my parents a few more years while completing high school and about a year after graduating, I got married and eventually moved to the United States.

Looking back, I can see that this was an escape of sorts from everything that was not able to be spoken out loud.

Moving away from my family achieved the one goal that my young, immature mind was focused on, and that was to get me away from my mother. I lost so much more than I could fathom from making that decision.

In my effort to get away, I ended up isolating myself from my dad, my brother, and my sisters. I'm sure you're not supposed have a favorite sibling, but my brother and oldest sister are my favorites. I missed them terribly.

I stopped calling and writing. I felt ashamed, guilty, angry, and every other emotion imaginable. I developed an attitude of, "I can do it all on my own," and that worked for me for a while, but it's interesting how having children of your own changes everything and gives you a different perspective on life in general.

I'm a firm believer that there are no coincidences in life and that everything happens for a reason. I believe that life events, situations, and people come into your life at the exact time that they are supposed to.

Whether we are ready for them or not, it's going to happen.

September 11th, 2001 was a huge turning point in my life. That was when the wheels of the, "I can take care of myself," wagon fell off.

I had to make some drastic changes in my life, had to stop putting band-aids on things and start dealing with past events. My mind and body were screaming for attention and could no longer handle being pushed back.

I weighed an all-time high of 260 pounds, my health was suffering terribly, I was stressed and suffered from severe anxiety. The only good things I felt I had in my life were my husband and my boys. I had left a trail of destruction behind me. A higher power was telling me that I had to start dealing with the stuff from my past. It was time to start feeling and healing.

The Game Changer

Have you ever heard the term, "when it rains it pours"? Well, I was in a full-blown hurricane!

My parents visit after my youngest son was born, pushed me over the edge. I loved seeing my parents read, play, and interact with my boys just as grandparents do. I still harbored hurt and anger towards my mother and kept everything very cold and clinical, as I always did. I never wanted to be alone with her for fear of losing it on her. I was too vulnerable, volatile, and very reactive!

Her visit ended in a huge argument that, in all honesty, had been brewing for a long time.

All the years of pent-up emotions came flooding out that night. I was crying, sobbing in fact, but I got everything out that I needed to say. Looking back, I must have looked like a crazy person. When you are hurting and have been hurting for so long, past events feel like they just happened, so they are still very fresh.

After I had unleashed everything on my mum, she simply told me that she didn't remember anything about the molestation and that she did the best she could as a parent.

I was shocked, to say the least, what a complete and total let down of a fight.

I had mentally rehearsed this conversation over and over in my head as to what I would say. All the way down to the nasty verbal jabs I would take at her to cause maximum pain. I wanted her to feel everything that I had felt and was stilling feeling.

I guess I was hoping to hear, "I'm sorry I didn't protect you," or some sort of explanation as to why she treated us the way she did.

Needless to say, the moment I had been waiting for was a massive let down.

I made her promise not to tell my dad or anyone in the family as I was ashamed of being molested. My mother agreed to not say anything and that was it.

Strangely, it was at that moment that I had a huge reckoning with myself. I realized that I was responsible for everything that had gone wrong in my life after I had left home; how I treated people, who I invited into my life, and how they treated me. I was responsible for my feelings and actions. I could no longer blame my mother for everything that had gone wrong in my life! I had used what had happened in my past as a crutch and allowed that to dictate how I made my decision, or as an explanation as to why things went wrong.

It was a very sobering moment and a very scary time. I had so much work to do to get my life back on track. I really wasn't sure where to start. It all seemed very overwhelming.

I had been walking around in victim mode being angry, overly tough and hard for so long because it was comfortable for me. That was my mechanism for coping.

Even though it was totally self-serving and not a healthy way to be, it was still comfortable. I had allowed this behavior to develop into a habit and it was going to be a hard one to break.

We develop habits in different ways and from different circumstances from responses to emotional situations, good and bad experiences, and generationally from how our parents did things. We are always receiving information; our brain deciphers this and then we respond. This then becomes our go-to response and then habits are created.

In some cases, the response is reactionary like the "Flight or Fight" response. In most cases though, we have a choice regarding how we respond.

I had to understand that concept first to be able to start the healing process. I read books, went to classes, and sought professional assistance with hypnotherapy.

I had created a few habits that helped me through tough situations in my past, but they were no longer serving me now. They had not been serving me well for a long time, but they were comfortable and familiar. Habits like pushing feelings and emotions to the back of my mind because I did not have time to deal with them. I did not have the time to break down or fall apart.

Believe it or not, that mindset and my habits did help me through a very tough period in my life. Obviously, not the recommended method of what to believe and tell yourself or action steps to take to get through hard times. I also recognize the path of hurt and destruction I left while having this mindset and the relationships, missed opportunities, and happiness that were denied.

It's interesting the things we tell ourselves during certain times in our lives to just get through, but just like karma, life has a way of circling around and dropping it all back on you when you least expect it. It confronts you with all those thoughts, feelings, and situations that you didn't have time for and says, "now it's time, ready or not!"

This might seem like a simple concept to some, but when I really embraced the fact that I had a choice on how I responded to things, it blew the doors wide open on all the possibilities I had yet to experience in my life.

You are probably wondering why I would choose to share such a deeply personal story. For someone who is introverted like me, this is a TMI (too much information) situation. This wasn't easy, but I do so with great humility and the truth is, I care about YOU!

Being able to open up and share, owning my story and where I came from, is incredibly healing and encouraging.

By revisiting my childhood, my past, it has allowed me to recognize and honor the difficult times but has opened my mind to receive the good experiences I also had as a child. These experiences were previously blocked and hidden away from me. My parents had situations and events that happened to them which formed their lives, their choices, and decisions. I have been able to take a step back and see truly that although we had some really bad situations and hardships, my parents did the best they could with what they had. I was able to see that my parents also created some fantastic experiences and were able to pass on some wonderful gifts and traits as well.

There are many of you out there who may have had a similar upbringing, or worse than mine. There may be some who are just going through the motions wondering if this is it, is this all life has to offer after everything you have been through.

I'm here to tell you, no, this is not it! Life has more to offer if you choose to allow it. You were not meant to live an ordinary life. You are meant to live an extraordinary life!

What has happened in our past, is exactly that, our past. What we choose to learn from it, what we choose to do with it, is up to you my friend.

I chose to forgive; I chose to forgive my mother! I had always heard the saying, "Forgiveness is more for you than the other person," but I never really understood it until I put it into practice.

I chose to forgive myself for holding myself in a space that was unhealthy and that I didn't deserve. I chose to stop punishing myself for the things that were out of my control and chose to forgive myself for my actions and the way I responded.

Forgiveness does not mean you are condoning other people's actions or behaviors; it doesn't mean that you've wiped the slate clean to allow people to treat you the same way again. Forgiveness is not a sign of weakness.

Forgiveness is powerful, it's love, it's kindness, it's tolerance, it's patience, it's understanding, and its acceptance.

Forgiveness takes the power out of a hurtful situation and creates magnificent freedom that is a gift to you. It allows us to take a step back and look at the whole picture instead of the little pieces. It is an acceptance of something that is a lesson in so many ways and allows us to move forward. It allows us to continue learning and growing and experiencing life the way it's supposed to be experienced in all its splendor and glory. Forgiveness is like a do-over, and there are no set numbers or age limitations.

My upbringing and the choices I've made have allowed me to be able to reach you today!

My question to you is, "Is there room in your life for forgiveness?" I truly hope so. Because the truth is, you deserve so much more, and I wish that for you.

Dedication:

This chapter is dedicated to my husband, Eric. You believed in me even when I didn't have the courage to do so myself. I couldn't have imagined a better role model and father for my boys, and a lover and better partner in crime to navigate this wondrous thing called life.

To my boys, Dustin and Spencer, you give me a reason to smile every day. You have grown into fine young men and continue to surpass my expectations. It has been the greatest privilege of my life to be your mum. Dream big, work hard and continue to offer a helping hand wherever you can. I love you like 5 & 6, 20 &10.

To my sister Tracy, I have watched you with pure admiration from afar. We don't get to choose our family, but if we did, I'd choose you, hands down, no questions asked. We certainly had our challenges growing up in our family, but I watched you navigate the hardship and challenges with grace, courage, and sheer tenacity. You are my hero.

To my brother Justin, I always felt your love and protection no matter where I lived or what country I am in. You are the epitome of what it is to be a man. I look at my boys and see so many aspects of you in them. I am proud to call you my brother.

Sheridan Wickens-Fogg

Sheridan Wickens-Fogg

Sheridan Wickens-Fogg grew up in Australia and moved to the United States in 1997, she lives in Colorado with her husband and two children.

She is the CEO and Founder of Aussie Girl Skin Spa & Aussie Girl Go and has been in the health and wellness industry for over 10 years. She has over 20 years of experience in mentoring, training, process and procedural development and compliance.

She is one of the top experts in her field, combining her extensive knowledge of anatomy, physiology, health, wellness, nutrition and skin in a uniquely well-rounded approach for men and women to feel empowered and live a healthy life filled with passion and purpose.

She has dedicated her life to supporting men and women in how they look and feel about themselves and has a natural ability in bringing out the best in you.

Research has shown that strong emotions cause changes in the biochemistry of the body. Simply said – your biography or your story creates your biology.

The Game Changer

Our beliefs dictate our experiences, and our experiences come from our beliefs. We must let go of the things that inhibit us in order to change. What is one thing you need to let go of in order to create and unleash the power within?

As a health & life coach, national speaker, educator, successful aesthetician, Sheridan brings her knowledge and expertise to her customers who have achieved massive success and sustainable, life-changing transformations.

When you change your habits, you change your life!

If you are interested in learning more go to www.aussiegirlgo.com/free and click on FREE COACHING CONSULTATION to book an appointment.
You can visit Sheridan at: www.aussiegirlgo.com
https://www.facebook.com/aussiegirlgo

To view Sheridan's video interview scan the QR Code below or click on this link: https://youtu.be/gl0AlBlpcX0

Sheridan Wickens-Fogg

Tragedy to Victory ... A Choice!

By Merri-jo Hillaker

We all have wonderful family memories as well as heart-wrenching ones. This memory encompasses my family's greatest tragedy yet shines a lasting light through it all. Hard to do? Absolutely! Yet, is it possible to gain strength through loss and move forward with stronger faith and love? Absolutely!

I was born into a poor family: four children in four years (all about 9 to 12 months apart excepting the miscarriage!). That's hard to believe, but my mother was born in 1920 and my dad in 1922, and they married at 30 and 28, respectively, so they took NO TIME in making those babies.

The first two were boys, Bill and Cliff. Then my sister Abbi showed up before I arrived last (and anything but least!). I loved my childhood – all the fun times we spent camping because we could not possibly afford hotels, and the trips to the woods with my "brothers" to catch frogs, snakes, and whatever wild bugs and animals would succumb to our relentless hunts! Thank goodness Mom had a sense of humor, as we were allowed to keep them all – even the squirrel that got loose in the basement!

I especially remember our mother sitting all 4 of us down in the playroom, then coming in with a cookie sheet upon which she had placed 8 or 10 miscellaneous objects (i.e., a cookie, a marshmallow, a pencil, a toy soldier, a ball, etc.). We were given a 10-second look at all the objects on the tray. Then she left the room, fully expecting us to write down on our pads of paper, every one of those items. What a game it was! We never knew that she was working diligently on our memories.

She also made me and Abbi learn how to sew and knit when we were youngsters, as her background as a dress designer for Junior House the 12 years before marriage made her quite qualified! I mean, we sewed all our Barbie doll clothes and then started sewing all our own school clothes as well as knitting all those sweaters which were many living in the state of Wisconsin. Our summers were spent buying expensive Marshall Field's dresses, taking them home and laying them out on bakery paper to make patterns, and then returning the dresses for refunds (as we couldn't afford to buy them in the first place). My sister still blames my mother for "ruining her life," as she stole all of our summers. I remember it quite differently: we were a poor family but, when it came to school, we looked like a million bucks!

My oldest brother and sister were genius-level (now referred to as "eggheads"). It wasn't as if Cliff and I were dumb, as I had graduated #3 of my high school; I was also among the top 10% of my undergrad and Order of Coif in law school. However, my sister and oldest brother's intelligence was such that it almost hindered their ability to make friends. So, Cliff and I became quite close. During high school, he would come in late at night, wiggle my foot to awaken me, and proceed to tell me about all his antics that evening. We saw each other often at high school parties that the other two would never attend. We were filled with lots of life and vigor, as well as very playful natures. I was never as funny as Cliff was, as he used his falsetto "to a T," cracking up everyone around him! Cliff never dated much, which was one area in which we differed from each other. I loved dating. However, he was kind of a protector of his younger sister as I found out by the stories that he told some young men who were pursuing me!

When college came around, we went our separate ways. I headed to UW – Madison and he attended Spencerian in Milwaukee. Still, we remained close and had a few adventures during the holidays at our parents' home. I specifically remember the time when I brought my then-fiancé home and Cliff brought home a homeless man whom he was counseling at church and who had nowhere else to celebrate the holiday. Why not the Lau house? At dinner, the guy took a liking to me and grabbed a carving knife, I believe to go after my fiancé. I fled to the "playroom," where I hid in the closet as my two brothers tackled this guy, breaking the window in the kitchen door, and wrestled the knife away. Again, my brother Cliff protected me.

When Cliff told me he was getting married, I was happy for him, although I really never got to know his wife-to-be. I am not sure how long they dated – maybe a year or so. Cliff seemed really happy and had not dated much throughout his earlier years. About a year later, they headed out to Multnomah Bible College in Oregon, where they both took classes. They returned to Milwaukee, where Cliff had a great job in sales... and then the first baby came along! Wow, David Josiah Lau, the apple of all our eyes! I was practicing law at Foley and Lardner at the time, but I well remember babysitting that little guy at about six months. I could not get him to stop crying! Forty minutes into it, after trying virtually everything, I put him in the kitchen sink. No kidding, he stopped crying! Well, I thought about writing a book on that, as clearly I never heard that method to quash a baby's tears. Thankfully, though, I never pursued it, as I am sure it had no chance of being a best-seller!

A couple of years later, Kathleen was restless and demanded that they move to Southern California. I remember financing their move, though only out of love for Cliff. Seeing the sacrifice he was making to keep her happy was upsetting to me. Cliff found another good job in sales in California and then along came another bundle of joy: Rene! We sure love her!

By the time David turned five, Kathleen was restless once again. Now the schools weren't good enough, so she forced the family to move yet again, causing Cliff to give up still another good job. This time, they went to Mammoth Lakes, California, in the beautiful Sierra Madres. It's a ski resort town. Cliff found a job as a condominium manager, so he was given a condominium as part of his compensation. He did okay and the kids really enjoyed the surroundings. Once again, it wasn't enough. Kathleen wanted a house. Well, there was not enough money for that, so she finagled the funds for the down payment from my parents by using a threat that they would never see their grandkids again. Kathleen moved in and took Rene, while David stayed with his dad. It wasn't the best situation by any means, plus Kathleen was running around with another man.

Finally, Cliff and Kathleen filed for divorce. Due to Kathleen's mental issues, for which they had gone to counseling, though nothing had ever worked, Cliff was awarded custody of the children. When Kathleen left town to go back to Southern California, she stole Rene. I received the call and told Cliff that I would hire a lawyer to get Rene back. Cliff's response was, "No! Better to have my kids apart and alive than dead."

Wow, that brought a chill to my bones. I tried to talk further but Cliff was really not too interested in sharing. I felt his shame.

So, the kids lived apart, seeing each other only during visitation. When I tried to take them all on vacation, whether to Belize on an archeological dig or to Alaska, Kathleen always interfered. Now they were getting into their teens: David was 14 and Rene was 12. In November 1997, I received a call from Cliff, who told me that he was thinking about getting back together with Kathleen. Oh my gosh, I had a lot to say. But Cliff believed it was what the Lord wanted. I was sick but had no comeback for that except "are you sure?" By April of the next year, they were remarried. The kids were finally together in Mammoth Lakes, living in the same house and attending the same school. All Cliff wanted was for his kids, who so loved each other, to be together.

Within a mere three months, Cliff and Kathleen were back in counseling. The crazy things I heard about from Cliff – things I had to pull out of him – were heart-wrenching. He was trying so hard. He even called and said that Kathleen was worried about the assets, which were all in Cliff's name, as I had helped Cliff buy a condo and house for financial security. He (really, she) wanted me to transfer them into her name. I could see what she was up to. Clearly, she regarded these investments as being part of her future financial security, although they belonged solely to Cliff, as they had been acquired when he was single. I put off that task until after Christmas. By the middle of January, Kathleen had moved back to Southern California, leaving the kids and Cliff behind. Things were calm...

Then I received the call ... Friday, April 27, 1998. Cliff had been killed – a gunshot to the head while at the condominium office. I knew immediately that it had to be her! I was so angry! I went to a friend's church, as I was out of town, and cried out to God, blaming Him for all of this. Clearly, there was a better way! Why would He let my brother, who was like Jesus, die such a horrific death? Why did He not take Kathleen, who was so very disturbed? There was no logic to this! I wept and cried out for over three hours, until I was truly spent. These two beautiful kids had now lost both parents to this dastardly act! "How, Cliff, was this better than having your children live apart and you be alive?" Of course, he could not answer!

The next morning, I awakened to find myself in this impossible state of peace... the one we read about, "the peace of God which passeth all understanding" Phil 4:7. Clarity overcame me, although sadness still took my breath and brought on massive tears. I was no longer hating my sister-in-law but truly allowing God to have His way with me. What would Jesus do? He would forgive if she were to ask for forgiveness. Matt. 6:14

What would I do? I was not bound by the need for her to be repentant. Perhaps we are called out through prayer and supplication to ask the Lord for forgiveness so that He shall forgive. I am to love as Christ loved. BUT not when this woman committed such a heinous act, right?

BUT, BUT, BUT... yes, a thousand buts. The huge challenge was really how to avoid "doubling down" on this awful, horrific murder that had already robbed me of my brother, that had robbed his two beautiful children of their loving father, and that had resulted in the loss of a godly man who loved everyone he ever came across on this earth? If I kept the poison of unforgiveness inside me, it would destroy me and my happiness. Also, it was clear that the children were going to move in with me. They were broken by the loss of both parents and now they would be moving away from the beauty of the Sierra Madres to the flat plains of Texas. Truly, what damage would my unforgiveness do to them?

The next day, as I drove from Reno after having flown in to get to Mammoth Lakes to handle the aftermath (thanking God every moment for my legal background), I found my car veering off the road in Bridgeport ... and going to visit Kathleen in jail. It was an amazing visit. I prayed with her, gave her some money, and moved on. As I got back on the road to Mammoth, I caught myself saying, "What the heck was that?!" Yes, recognizing how impossible it was to do, yet with God anything is possible.

The kids moved to Dallas a month later at the end of school. We had a huge rummage sale for all the things they chose not to keep and then we drove the rental truck for two days, from those incredible, beautiful mountains in the Sierra Madres to the boring flatlands of Texas. I told them about my journey to forgiveness. I said that when they could find it in their heart, I wanted them to start flying out to visit their mom in prison. They would only ever have one mom, but I made it clear that as their "auntie," I would raise them as if I had birthed them, with all the love I could give them. Within 18 months, they were flying out to California to see their mom.

Both Rene and David never acted out or exhibited and unusual behavior, but they had some depression from time to time, especially during that first summer. It was not easy, but I spoke of their father often, what he meant to me and to the world. I loved and continue to love these kids (now mature adults) as if they were mine... because, honestly, they are! God's first, Cliff's second, and then mine! David never dated much in college and every relationship seemed to end, so Auntie was a bit worried. I was concerned that his mother's behavior would stifle his ability to have a meaningful relationship with any woman. But then he found her... the one God had chosen. Today, they have a beautiful two-year-old son, Logan, and another one coming in November. Rene is happily married with a great job and a beautiful house in Frisco. You would never guess that their childhoods had been marred by that incredible tragedy. Although it is something they will forever carry, they both know that God is in control, and their loss is only temporary.

The walk of forgiveness is an optional one. We have a choice. But the incredible pain and sadness that unforgiveness brings, the never-ending heartache, is so incredibly costly. It is truly "doubling down" on a traumatic event that has already robbed us of something beautiful. Why is it that we continue allowing it to rob us... of joy, of peace, of a sense of equity and fairness, of truly living? Is it because of our "need to be right?" Our need to punish and retaliate? Trust me when I say "You will never win that battle, but it will continue to destroy you."

Notice where those needs come from and always keep the perspective that carrying it is like poison in your system. It is doubling down on an already grievous loss. We were not called to understand all that happens on this earth, but we were called to love one another as Christ loves us! When you can find this peace after an event as awful as this, you can truly find peace in anything. It is the peace beyond understanding. I pray that if you are carrying unforgiveness, especially for yourself, that you, too, can reach out, let go, and re-establish the love that is within to create what you were called to do, and to make a difference in this world of ours which so desperately needs to hear your voice!

The Game Changer

Merri-jo Hillaker

Merri-jo Hillaker was a woman driven to achieve all that is possible, being born 4th of four children in a poor Wisconsin family. She graduated with honors and double degrees from the University of Wisconsin, then graduated top 10% from both the University of Wisconsin Law School with her JD, and New York University School of Law with a Master's in Taxation.

Merri-jo practiced law at Foley and Lardner in Milwaukee, and after 3 years was hired away as Vice President General Counsel of a publicly-traded company at 28 years old.

Pursuing her entrepreneurial spirit, she moved to Texas in her 30's where she successfully purchased and ran businesses, two of which produced 7 figure results for her, while at the same time continued to provide legal services which she does today but only on a charitable basis, helping those less fortunate.

She is totally committed to helping people build passive income as she has become an avid investor herself. When her father became very ill in the early 1990s, she found herself developing and pursuing yet another passion, health and wellness. She now runs her 25+-year-old health and nutrition company, and recently added another business fulfilling yet another great passion of hers which is self-development. Through her Global Mindset Mastery Association, she supports others to break through their limiting beliefs, as she says, *"the things you don't know you don't know"*, so that they too can live totally fulfilling lives.

Her heart is bigger than the State of Texas, and her goal is to touch a million lives! Her question to you, *"How can I best support you?"*

For more information or to contact Merri-jo,
www.merrijohillaker.com
mj@merrijohillaker.com

To view Merri-jo's Game Changer Video scan the QR code below or click on this link: https://youtu.be/RW2xhRhQM7Y

Escaping My Safety Zone

By Carolyn Ortman

The night before the big trip, Scott called. His brother was sick and since I was the only other one with rafting experience, he asked me to guide the second raft. I hesitated because I'd only been on guided trips—never as the guide. Wanting to help, he convinced me it wouldn't be that difficult. If he thought I could do it, then I could!

Scott's annual rafting trip was down the South Fork of the American River, a Class III river. I'd been on more rigorous rivers. Most of our group expressed their nervousness as we boarded the boats—Scott leading one and me the other. Off we went on our fun adventure! The rapids weren't that tough, or so I thought, getting a little too comfortable. The first rapid was pretty tame, but the second was more ferocious. I was unable to stabilize my feet so with the first bounce, I went into the cold river.

I floundered to catch my breath, scraping my hands through the water to grab onto anything. Part of my body hit a rock. Finally, I got to the raft and the members helped me up. I saw them grimace just as I felt a throbbing pain in my knee. I had a big gash with what looked like visible bone. Luckily, two nurses were on the trip! They did what they could as we traveled through more rapids for medical attention. Instead of enjoying the trip, I was in pain. Sadly, my days as a rafting guide were over. Even worse, I felt I let Scott down.

Most of my life I played it safe, but how many people would:

- Take on roaring rapids or skydiving.
- Travel overseas leading business training sessions—sometimes on unfamiliar topics.
- Start a business with little money AND no business plan!
- Go through an intensive personal and professional development certification program as the only female trainee.

I took these opportunities on without much forethought.

That's how a lot of my life has been—rolling in and out of what I call my "Safety Zone." I will throw caution to the wind taking on adventures and activities like those listed above—sometimes just because someone like Scott believed I could. More often, I would hold back when it got too scary. I'd recoil to my safe place, often overthinking the situation, and live from my head in lieu of trusting my "gut."

I am now a master trainer, a marketing expert with an MBA, run my own marketing and training business, and have been an independent entrepreneur for over 13 years. I've delivered over 1200 presentations, programs, and training worldwide to corporate, small business, and higher education audiences. I am more content in my own skin and more aligned with my core values. This didn't happen overnight—and I'm still learning and growing. It's ironic that I've always encouraged my students to develop their core values, but I wavered on my own. When I finally got serious and listened to my own advice, things changed for me.

I'm much more comfortable now proclaiming that I am a business owner, recognizing that it's necessary to admit what I don't know and to ask for help. I wasn't always like this. Like many, I have my corporate past. I'd like to say it was a stable, secure environment, but I can't. My drive and my passion to learn and share with others kept me going.

Why Was I in My Safety Zone?
Beyond the occasional awkward hug, there was no regular exchange of emotions in my family. Even the infrequent "I love you" was strained. This impacted my life in ways I didn't understand until later.

Vulnerability was not my strong suit. I would rather do it myself, even struggle at times, than admit I needed help and support.

As the younger daughter, Mom sheltered me. Later, she would tell me:
- "Fake it till you make it."
- "Never let them see you sweat."
- "Don't air your dirty laundry."

For example, at one of my first jobs as an advertising copywriter, I was placing an ad on a colleague's desk after hours when I saw some hurtful comments she had shared about me with a co-worker. Although very juvenile as if I was back in high school, it still hurt. I called Mom for a kind word and support. She listened, waiting until I could clear my tears. She felt bad, but instead of consoling me, she reminded me that not everyone will be our friends and to "buck it up." This came from a woman who years later was more worried about bothering her neighbors with a noisy ambulance siren than getting care for her broken hip!

The Journey Begins...

My journey as a small business owner and entrepreneur began by happenstance. At my first real job after college, I worked for Michael Gerber, author of *The E-Myth*, at their Southern California office. Even though I worked on the operations side, I learned through interactions with the client services staff about the struggles small business owners face. Michael was passionate about providing the knowledge and motivation to these owners by offering a more formulated, systematized approach that many larger businesses, like McDonald's, had already adopted. *I didn't see the true value in his philosophy, however, until I was a business owner myself.*

When I settled into my first managerial position, I thought I had arrived! With Dad an artist and my sister owning a personal training business, I was going to be the family member who worked in a *real* corporate job. I'd put in my time, rise through the ranks, and retire from that job with a nice nest egg. Sounded good!

Instead, I started to feel out of place. I didn't understand what was happening. *I didn't trust my gut or see the red flags.* The manager who hired me was retiring. It seemed like I couldn't work enough hours to keep up with the new pace and expectations.

Working late one night, a colleague and I started chatting about her weekend plans and we got on the topic of the future. Out of the blue, I blurted out, "Madeline, do you ever feel like there's more to life than this?" She responded, "Whatever, Carolyn," with a perplexed look which made me quickly change the subject.

Instances like this made it difficult for me to trust and build relationships with colleagues. By delving back to my safety zone, my colleagues and friends didn't get to know the real me—the loving, fun, energetic, creative me just waiting to escape.

"You No Longer Have a Job."

None of us want to hear these words, but many have. When the shock wore off, I felt some stress and relief slowly melt away. No longer would I need to face the day in uncertainty and trepidation. Yet, there was a new reality: *No job meant no income.* I spun out of control until my anxiety hit the upper limit. Prior Dale Carnegie training on handling worry and stress helped me put the situation in perspective and live in "day-tight compartments."

Don't look too far into the future.

Instead, live the day that is right in front of you.

I learned that even under unfathomable stress, I was stronger than I realized, but I remained in my safety zone. My attempt to "move on" came with a new corporate position as a marketing director that was over 100 miles from home. I crafted the perfect plan: I'd rent a room near work, my boyfriend would live at my house, and we'd enjoy our weekends together! This sounded great, but later I came to realize that I was running from a truth, a nagging voice inside my head that I refused to face: **corporate was not the place for me!**

Ken, the hiring manager, had confidence in me, "I really think you can do this job." Focusing on his strong challenge, I missed him mentioning the string of individuals who previously held this marketing director position in a short time. As had been, and would be, my motto for years:

If someone believes I can do it, then I can!
I made progress evaluating the 20+ marketing and sales department personnel, even with their negative attitudes. I took actions gaining their trust, but that job lasted less than a year. My gut told me I didn't belong there because the owners, who expressed their need for change, weren't adaptive.

Although anxious about job hunting, I recognized that I had tried something new and different. I had taken on several challenges—a new geographic area, a new way to live, and a new way to flex my managerial muscle. I had definitely lived beyond my safety zone!

Fast forward to a new government transportation job in Orange County as a marketing program manager. My good friend Freddie commented, "Well, they can't lay you off. It's government! You'll be there as long as you want." Two years later, I was laid off.

My more "spiritual" friends insisted my layoff was a "sign," but I wasn't buying it! A sign for what? That's when I heard again, "You really need to start living from your heart and to start asking "the universe" for guidance." How? I'd just been in a government position mired with analysis, rules, and regulations.

Opening Up
When I was laid off, I was volunteering as a crisis center hotline counselor in Orange County. When Mom inquired as to why I wanted to volunteer in such a capacity, I blurted out, "Because I want to help people who are hurting."

This experience opened me up—and my heart. One night, I was listening to a woman share her anguish over her abusive relationship with her boyfriend. At times, she was sobbing so intensely her speech was inaudible. I felt uncomfortable, but my training was all about listening, so I did just that. By the end, she seemed more relaxed and settled. She then asked, "Who are you people?" having no idea whom she had called. She had just dialed the first number that might help her.
My heart started to feel heavy.

Was this the "living from your heart" concept to which my friends had been referring? Just before my last day in government, I found myself chatting with the finance manager about future employment possibilities. He mentioned the living speakers make sharing their wisdom. It seemed ridiculous to me that people could make a career by just speaking. Little did I know that I would challenge myself, step out of my safety zone, and be making money speaking many years later!

There and Back Again

Carolyn Ortman

Becoming a pro in job search techniques (which I would later teach to others), my resumé was beginning to look like Swiss cheese with all the holes. I needed to fill those holes!

I auditioned for contract training with a global seminar company. Years before, I had become a certified Dale Carnegie instructor. I wanted to determine if I still had my "training edge."

Before I fully threw myself into this work, I visited my local Inland Empire Women's Business Center. When I shared my marketing background with the director, she told me her clients could use marketing services encouraging me to start my own business. That sounded like a huge undertaking. I just wanted to find work that would pay my bills.

I hit the road as a trainer, traveling worldwide, delivering 1-2 day seminars. It wasn't uncommon to train 4-5 days in a week, visiting that same number of airports while sometimes driving close to 200 miles between cities. I was sent to Australia, New Zealand, and the United Kingdom (UK).

My very first overseas assignment was to the UK for 14 consecutive days, in 14 separate regions, teaching conflict management skills for women. My boyfriend insisted on showing me on the map how expansive a trip I would be taking. With both excitement and trepidation, I took off for this adventure, even though I had never traveled alone for that long.

After landing at Heathrow, I walked into the restroom, looked into the mirror, and thought, "I am completely alone—I don't know anyone in this entire country." I imagined my more extroverted counterparts thinking, "I can't wait to meet new people and have new experiences." Instead, my inner fear said, "I hope I get through this!" My smaller voice said, "Just go have fun!"

Often, my training crowds exceeded 100 participants. I had to warm to the culture (and they to me), speak to not offend, and sell support products, but they weren't buying. I made it through by believing in myself and setting aside my ego.

My years of travel training expanded my safety zone teaching me:

- To fix problems in and out of the training sessions including dealing with public transportation, trying to eat healthy, and helping participants become better at managing their challenges from marketing to communications to leadership.
- To research, organize, systematize, and process information quickly. *(Very valuable when I DID start my own business).*
- To challenge myself. to conquer fear of the unknown—large audiences, traveling, selling.
- To construct engaging training sessions to hold audiences' interests.
- To deal with rejection and fears.
- To be resilient, vulnerable, and not take things personally.

Breaking Away…But Slowly
Have you ever stayed in something too long—a relationship, a job, or other situation even though you knew you were done? Well, seven years into contract training, I was actually "done"—at least emotionally and mentally. I continued for 5 more years because it was comfortable, familiar, and safe. I started to make small changes to break away.

For example, while attending a sales/marketing conference, I agonized that there are plenty of marketing businesses out there. *Why should I be just one more?* The leader, Ursula Mentjes, told me, "No one delivers marketing like you do, Carolyn. You are unique."

I wrote an award-winning business plan and joined a business mastermind group that heavily encouraged me to launch my own programs. I launched some, and things went well, but I gave no time for the momentum to build. I felt disappointed and frustrated. More fear had cropped up! I went from being courageous to fearful again—back to my safety zone.

My inner voice started to get stronger saying, "More businesses need to experience your gifts of marketing." Even though a colleague encouraged me to be a marketing coach, I had run from that "label" thinking it wasn't a legitimate job. I recalled what Ursula had said years before about being unique.

Several years later, I was talking to Bob Henry, a SCORE counselor, about the multitude of programs and projects I had worked on and developed since leaving "cubicle life." He provided sound words of encouragement, "Carolyn, the only challenge I see with you is you lack FOCUS." He wrote FOCUS on the face of his business card and handed it to me. That was the prompt I needed to go beyond my safety zone and do my own work. Today, Bob's card is still pinned to my office wall!

My final attempt to "go back" to a corporate job came, strangely, with tears of sadness. One day in the grocery checkout line, I picked up a voicemail inviting me back for a second interview. I had tears of disappointment instead of joy.

My Safety Zone Escape!

My favorite quote is:
If you want something you've never had,
you must be willing to do something you've never done."
                    —Thomas Jefferson

I add: "and be willing to be someone you've never been."

I was ready to commit to making a change—to *authentically* be someone who would do things differently. I would focus on creating my own marketing programs which meant reaching out and asking for help!

What made the difference?
- Starting daily habits and becoming more disciplined with my time. With a morning routine, my day became more positive and productive.
- Being willing to admit what I didn't know.
- Recognizing that vocalizing my accomplishments isn't bragging.
- Investing more heavily into my business and myself (Beware: Spending money to "fix" your business won't work long-term unless you "fix" yourself first).
- Working with mentors who instilled a larger vision in me.
- Realizing that fear takes on many forms including distraction and procrastination.

- Meditating regularly.
- Joining GirlFriendCircles and expanding my female friendships.
- Making a choice to live life via courage instead of fear.

I've been a student of personal and professional development work since college, but I haven't always applied what I learned. What finally started to stick was consistently focusing my learning in one area: mindset. Tony Robbins says that 80% of our success is due to our psychology. I interpret that as my mindset about myself and my future.

It's easy for us to get hijacked by our old "stories" reverting to our comfortable ways. We say we want change, but do very little to make it happen. We don't commit!

You can see that for many years I was a "reluctant entrepreneur." While I enjoy things like river rafting, I wasn't one who took risks in business. I saw entrepreneurs as risk-takers full of ideas. That wasn't me, or so I thought! The lessons we need to learn are often right in front of us, but it may take a while for us to act on them. We just have to open our eyes! Today, as I take my learnings to work with business owners and entrepreneurs, I understand that we may want to control our destiny—I did! The more we try to "force it," the more we are met with resistance and feelings of fear and insecurity. This process won't happen overnight. As Denzel Washington said,

"Without commitment, you'll never start, but more importantly, without consistency, you'll never finish."

Take one small step right now! And tomorrow, take another.

Carolyn Ortman

Carolyn Ortman, MBA

Since walking away from the cubicle life, Carolyn has passionately *steered businesses through the confusing maze of marketing choices to increase revenue and create their impact on the world.*

She is CEO of CKO Marketing Group—a firm that focuses on marketing and branding strategies through coaching, training and formulating business alliances. Clients learn how to reach their target market, craft messages that attract their ideal audiences and convert leads into sales.

Carolyn's signature programs, workshops, and individual training's have helped small business owners and entrepreneurs monetize their marketing, so they increase their bottom line. *Her focus is on branding, marketing strategy, customer service, and leadership practices.*

Her latest program, Client Attraction Blueprint, teaches businesses and individuals how to stand out and get found in the marketplace, while attracting the right clients.

With an MBA in Marketing, Carolyn draws from more than 20 years of business expertise and over 1200 training workshops and presentations. Carolyn is a sought-after speaker, master trainer, business coach, and marketing expert. She is also an adjunct instructor for the University of California at Riverside Extension Program and is an award-winning Toastmasters speaker.

To learn more about her:
www.CKOmarketing.com
Carolyn@CKOMarketing.com
951.256.4864

To view Carolyn's interview for The Game Changer, scan the QR Code below or follow this link: https://youtu.be/sWoqPdlDajA

Carolyn Ortman

A Life Worth Living

By Joey Nichols

The inmate sucker punched me while I was trying to calm down the situation. I was stunned by the impact when yet another blow hit my face. I managed to grab him, and we wrestled until he got the better of me. He began to push me over, but I took him to the ground with me. He rolled off me, stood up and yelled, "I'm going to kill you!" then lunged forward towards me trying to get close enough to strike. I lay on my back on the ground in a defensive pose and kicked him as he tried to reach me.

He tried again and I used my feet to keep him at a distance; something I had learned from an old film documentary I'd seen years earlier. The next time I kicked, he grabbed my boot and started to drag me backwards across the prison dorm. "I'm going to kill you!" he yelled again. I tried to grab onto something to keep from being dragged behind the back wall where, once out of sight of witnesses, he would presumably murder me. But I couldn't get a grip on any of the metal bunk beds lining the prison dorm and he kept pulling me back. The squeaking of our boots against the waxed floor echoed loudly as 48 other men stood by and watched. I was almost to the back wall and I was powerless to stop it.

Let me tell you how it got to this point…

Today, I am a happy and well-adjusted guy. I work for myself and I love what I do, so, I work a lot. Becoming an entrepreneur gave me so much more than just a new job title. Entrepreneurship gave me the confidence to also pursue my other dreams. Entrepreneurship became a way for me to make an impact on the world and share my hopes with others.

I also make the time to pursue my hobbies: I'm a musician, actor, public speaker, and volunteer. I have great friends and I try to be a great friend too. Life has become stable. But it hasn't always been so well balanced.

The road to self-actualization was not easy. It has been filled with pain, self-discovery, setbacks, fear, hope, and wonder.

I look back at photos of myself playing in the yard wearing a Superman cape and I have to admit that I was a cute kid. My home life was good, and I dreamed of being an adventurer, a musician, an actor, someone who was able to share their passion with the world. I got along with my friends and things were fine, but then I changed schools. When I started at the new school, I began to get the feeling that I wasn't good enough. I was passionate about so many things, but I was too shy to express myself. I felt embarrassed and assumed that others would judge me as harshly as I judged myself. I was picked last for sports. The other kids shamed me for wearing shoes I thought were cool but apparently didn't fit in with their standards. I was punished socially for being myself. I felt weird. I felt like I had no purpose in life. I was a wanderer.

I couldn't be one of the cool kids, so I made the decision to be the complete opposite. I met friends who did drugs and I tried them. Drugs made me feel like I had found the solution to life. I was running away from myself, but I couldn't get far enough away. Drugs made me feel like I was finally able to measure up. All the missing pieces were put back together again. I was invigorated and excited and I sought to feel that way as often as possible. To my surprise, life still had challenges and I still had feelings of insecurity and a lack of confidence. Self-doubt loomed like a shadow in the back of my mind. Every time I came down from drinking and using, I was stuck facing myself again. I rejected myself before others could. It hurt less that way. I began to use greater amounts and harder drugs to push back those feelings and to run away from myself to avoid facing my insecurities. My friends were all on that same path, but I was racing ahead of them in first place towards destruction.

Looking back, I can see that my friends liked me despite my troubles, but because they were troubled too, I thought they only liked me for those behaviors. I felt alone and thought that no one liked the real me. I could only find my voice and be okay when I was high. Opportunities to change my behavior and pursue my dreams presented themselves over and over again, but I couldn't find the courage and confidence to take advantage of them. I was full of self-pity and I was depressed.

The Game Changer

The drug use got worse and worse and my self-destruction reached new levels of degradation. I injected meth to stay up for days so I could hustle and get heroin. I injected heroin to function and numb the misery of existing.

I had been high and up for a week when a friend and I got arrested. I was terrified and empty and had no idea what to expect. I was 19 years old and weighed 120 lbs.

Finally, I ended up in prison facing 10 years for stealing a taxicab driver. I walked in there not knowing if I would be beaten, raped, or even murdered.

The pressure, stress, and fear I faced in there every day left me broken. I wanted to change but I couldn't see any way out of the mess I was in. The other inmates were constantly screaming, stealing, and arguing. The guards were cruel and verbally abusive and made life hell. It felt like I was drowning in time and I wanted to die. At least that was what I thought until I found myself being dragged back there to meet my fate.

That day I was dragged back to die, my bunkmate, who garnered some respect in the dorm, actually begged my captor not to hurt me. My bunkmate was a drug dealer from Atlanta, and he was the one who stopped the other inmate from ending my life that day. I had always offered him food or advice when he needed a little help. You never know how the kindness and investment you put into another person can come back to you. That was the first time I truly realized that I had to make a change immediately or I might not get another chance.

Afterward, another prisoner friend who was well connected heard about the incident and he offered to have his crew go take care of the guy that hit me - that is if I wanted him to. Part of me really did want him to, because I felt scared and humiliated and embarrassed and mad and confused. Plus, people were pressuring me to drop a padlock into a sock and use it to beat him in the head. If I was willing to do that, next time people wouldn't think I was an easy target. This was an opportunity to have someone else take care of my problem for me.

I had started to learn a little self-help and spiritual guidance by this time, and I had practiced enough so that I was able to pause and think about what I wanted for my future. For the first time in a long time, I felt in touch with my true self. I told him no, I wanted to let it go. I started to hang around other people who were seeking to get better. I attended all the counseling classes that were available. I had spent years running from myself, but it was finding myself that finally opened the door to my redemption.

I got out of prison and got help for my addiction and major issues. That was necessary before I could tackle some of the deeper-rooted problems that drove me to use in the first place. There were setbacks, but over time I was able to get a firm grip on sobriety.

I found mentors who volunteered their time and energy. They introduced me to a new perspective on life. There was still much to learn, and if I wasn't sure if I could do it, but they showed me love and compassion and they told me that they believed in me. They said that I was a winner, despite what my current circumstances looked like because I was taking action to expand my life. I decided to try.

Over the next few years, I worked hard and made connections. I adopted the mindset of being helpful and interested in other people. I took the time to seek ways to add value to their lives. I began to take bold imperfect actions and made massive progress. I opened up a massage and personal training company, co-founded a real estate investment company, became a character actor on the most-watched TV show in the world, studied audio engineering, and then recorded and produced over 30 of my own songs.

A big part of my success has come from learning early on to invest in myself and be open to new opportunities when they appear. Every day, we use our energy on something in our lives. We can either remain unintentional and let it be scattered, or we can focus our energy on our self-improvement thus creating change. I am relentless in this aspect.

At first, simply resisting the bad habits was enough. But I found that I could not be happy while staying stagnant. I had to replace the old behaviors and beliefs with positive habits. As time passed and my relationship with myself deepened, I started to dive deeper into personal development and spiritual growth. I began to implement success habits; things like meditation, daily routines, time management, nightly growth inventories, etc.

I found what I had been seeking in the outside world was already deep within me the entire time. I just needed guidance and a step by step plan to work through my mess and get to know myself. I needed to take focused daily actions that enabled me to step into my new identity.

I became more confident and able to look the world in the eye without blinking. I dared to take bigger risks and pursue bigger dreams. I helped others to get to know themselves and to map out the actions they need to take to become who they wanted to be and have a life they could consider a success; a life worth living. Helping others made me feel connected and fulfilled. Seeing those same faces become filled with hope and joy has given me a purpose. Entrepreneurship gave me a vehicle and the space that fulfills my need for creativity, variety, challenge, etc. It helps me to reach others already working on their lives but still missing those pieces on the inside. I can show them how to smash through their self-imposed inner stumbling blocks and rip away self-doubt and fear so that they can experience inner freedom that shifts into external success.

I am passionate about my belief that no one should let a lack of confidence and fear hold them back from living a successful life. Because I spent so much of life trapped, I am passionate about helping people find inner peace.

When someone is living a life that is not true to their values, it can be hidden from the outside world; yet deep inside, they know. It seems easier to numb out those feelings through drugs, alcohol, sex, work, exercise or TV, but the results are temporary. Lasting fulfillment comes through change.

So many people waste their lives running from themselves as I did. People die because they haven't been shown how to overcome their shame and confidence issues and they numb their pain until nothing is left. It can be that severe.

On the flip side, once the issues have been overcome, those people can inspire others and show them how to grow and add more hope to the world. They can make a deposit in the hope bank and the interest we gain when investing in making someone's life better never goes away. The challenges I face today are of a much higher quality than they once were.

My relationships, my finances, my living situation, my sense of integrity, my relationship with myself, my discipline, my interests, my interest in other people – all of this has evolved over time. I have this borrowed time in the world now because I asked for help and pursued the solution that was offered to me. I stayed open-minded and curious. I never stopped learning and I never stopped searching and I won't quit.

Now I have a mission and a step by step process to turn it into a reality. And again, that's what I want for you. I am now a voice for those who no longer have one and for those who still don't know there is hope beyond their current situations. It brightens my day to see the light come on in someone's eyes, to see them start to rock their lives and own their voice. I love watching them discover that they too are capable of doing extraordinary things that at one time they would never have thought possible.

All real change starts with changing ourselves- whether it's the internal dialogue and bad habits that limit us or finding a mentor to guide us into being the best physical and mental version of ourselves – you are not alone. Every day more people take action to reach their goals. We can do this together.

The Game Changer

Joey Nichols - UpLift Your Life Academy

Joey Nichols is an Atlanta-based entrepreneur and dream chaser. His journey of transformation began during his life's lowest point- amidst heroin addiction, suicide attempts, and a prison sentence. He was broken and hopeless until he found a mentor and discovered a path of personal and spiritual development that changed everything and made a new life possible. This practical spiritual solution gave him a new start and new-found freedom to make his dreams a reality. Determined to pave his own way to success, he dove head-first into personal development and business education.

At age 26, Joey started his first business and over the next several years became an accomplished life coach, health & fitness expert, actor, model, inspirational speaker, and advocate for suicide prevention and recovery from substance abuse. His work, his coaching, and his willingness to unflinchingly share his story of hope has inspired and helped hundreds create lasting breakthroughs around their health and well-being. He's passionate about building community and helping others to discover their own path to inner freedom, confidence, and success.

When he is not focused on his business, Joey is usually playing and recording music, writing poetry, or practicing mixed martial arts. He has an easy-going sense of humor and is quick to smile and brighten someone else's day.

Joey Nichols

Connect with Joey
Web: UpLiftYourLifeAcademy.com
Email: support@upliftyourlifeacademy.com
Instagram: @joeyjafar
LinkedIn: linkedin.com/in/jn-atl

To view Joey's interview for the Game Changer, scan the QR Code below or click on this link: **https://youtu.be/jgyM4n_SyhM**

Don't Be a Victim – Be a Victor!

By Toni Kaufman

In December of 2010, my life changed forever. While on a family trip to Tokyo Disney we fell in love with Japan. I noticed that not only were my son and I taller than most people we encountered, but in the subways, trains, and open walkways, everyone wore a mask. I wondered if I should be wearing one. What was the reason? Being a good American tourist, I never bothered to ask or find out. We were only there for seven days and what could possibly happen? I wish I had asked.

When I returned home, I developed a dry hacking cough, but in Houston, that's par for the course due to allergies, bad air, and the numerous spores in the air, so I thought nothing of it. By February, the cough had caused me to have headaches then my ribs started hurting from my excessive coughing. Eventually, not two minutes would go by without that infernal coughing attack. What was causing this, Asthma, Bronchitis, Pneumonia? Seven different doctors that I met with gave me a plethora of diagnosis and medication for this cough.

On March 7th, 2011, I gave my husband "the look" after I heard my rib snap during a coughing attack, and we headed to the ER. Fourteen days later, after a Bronchoscopy, I was diagnosed with H1N1 or as it's often called, Swine Flu. From one day to the next my ICU room was visited by aliens in HazMat suits telling me I was going to be okay. Thirty-seven days later I was finally able to go home. But I went home in a wheelchair, weighing in at about 206 lbs. mainly from intravenous steroids and steroid-induced Diabetes. I was weak, unable to walk, now had scarred lungs, and liver, and a highly compromised immune system.

Through the grace of God, and much physical therapy, I came back to fight another day. I recovered, returned to work, and learned how to maintain a normal life. I was hired by HP, fell in love with the people of the company, rose through the ranks to become Chief of Staff of Global IT - SAP Technologies, and then worked with some great people doing employee engagement and communications.

On Thursday, April 7th, 2014, my friends and family gave me a "20th Anniversary of my 39th birthday," party and over 30 people showed up. It was amazing! The next day, Friday, I felt a cold coming on, so I went to the doctor, got the usual treatment for that type of symptom, and spent the weekend trying to get well. by Monday, I was in the ER again. By Tuesday, my trachea and my lung had collapsed. Here we go again. Ten days later, I was on the disabled list again. Thank you H1N1 leftovers!

You see, you don't really heal from this type of a boxing match. The one-two punch you get delivered is a tough hit for someone my age. So, here's the plan, when you get dealt with this type of blow, you learn how to breathe again. You learn how to walk again, and you spend time researching and learning what it takes to fight it. You immerse yourself in research studies from Johns Hopkins and from people who know how to rebuild immune systems. You survive. If you so choose.

This entire episode in my life, from being sick to being fired for being sick, is why I chose to write *"ACT 2: Your Show Must Go On"*. I wanted to bring light, hope, and healing to those of us I like to call, 'America's Walking Wounded'.

THE DEATH OF THE AMERICAN DREAM

"They chew you up and spit you out, is it possible that the American Dream is dead?" -Toni Kaufman

What was the American dream? You go to school, you work hard, go to college, do well, graduate, and get a good job. You move up the corporate ladder until one day you retire and live happily ever after.

From my paths and passages, choices, energy, and passion, I knew that when I personally experienced being laid off, after working hard for most of my life, the story I just shared with you, of my family vacation ending up with my getting H1N1 and having to spend 37 days in the hospital. I took sick leave and was quickly asked to come back to work and they promised to accommodate my handicap created by the disease. I gave up my company plan for long-term disability and went back to work. But less than three months later, they laid me off.

If I had remained on long term disability, I would have kept over 75% of my salary for at least 18 months. Now, that option was gone. I felt cheated and ripped off at a time when I truly believed they would help me, and I needed their help more than ever. Once I was laid off, I lost my life insurance and health insurance due to the high cost of COBRA. I was pretty much on my own.

You see, when big corporations lay people off, they give you a package. This package normally includes counseling and training by a corporation that gives you lessons on how to rewrite your resume, how to answer the right questions, how to try and try and try until you give up trying to find another job. It was a dreadful, embarrassing, meaningless, time which I spent trying to play the game and see if I could be hired by someone, anyone, again.

I found myself walking into a conference waiting room with about six or seven men and women in their grey suits all looking and feeling like they had been kicked in the teeth. We were coached by people less than half our age and got schooled on how to do what we knew to do to get rehired. I just knew I couldn't retire; I was not ready. I was 57 years old and no one would hire me. I sent out well over 200 resumes. I even reached out to friends and family, but nothing proved fruitful. It was an exercise in futility and humility. These feelings of hopelessness and depression are precisely why I felt the need to share what I learned and experienced with you. You see this type of experience leaves you shaken to your very core. All areas of your life are affected; the body, the mind, your spiritual, and physical well-being are all devastated. What happened to me can be verbalized as feeling unconnected to my purpose and my chosen field of work as well as my personal choices.

Let's assume that you are one of us, America's Walking Wounded. The sooner that you face it, the sooner you begin to heal. Particularly with my group of Baby Boomers, raised by the Greatest Generation, we were taught to keep a "stiff upper lip." You just have to hang in there. Be strong. Survive.

All of these things are true. But a genuine disconnect lies between these mechanisms and actually having the inner capacity for real change. Anyone can act like they are OK, or they are going to be OK. Did anyone ever mention that "hanging in there," and "being strong," was easier said than done? The truth is that for most, these things can be inwardly impossible with the level of anxiety that comes with losing a long-time job. It's is truly life-changing.

"Life is what happens when you're busy making other plans"
-John Lennon

We are calling on you to reach deep into the darkness that has befallen you, acknowledge it, embrace it, attack it, accept it in as much as you acknowledge that it happened and resolve to deal with it in some way, shape, or form, realizing that you have no real idea, just yet, how in the hell you are going to do that. And that would be OK.

Contrary to corporate belief, life is a journey. Not a destination. It is time for you to begin a fearless inventory.

- Realize that you are a consequence — not a victim.
- Resolve to never, ever, ever give up and give in to victimhood.
- Refuse to allow yourself to be hobbled.
- Refuse to wallow in self-pity.
- Refuse to have your circumstances dictated to you by the callous actions of others.

Blame does not matter anymore. Fault does not matter anymore. What matters is moving forward. Moving past these circumstances. Adapting to what you have been handed. And yes, getting over it.

- Laugh, cry, yell, scream, see a counselor.
- Consult your spiritual advisor. Get a tarot card reading.
- Take a really long walk.
- Do pushups and sit-ups until you feel like you are going to vomit.
- Attend an AA meeting so that you can see the very essence of inner struggle in someone else.
- Visit a hospital or nursing home where there are sick and

dying, where you can see with your own eyes that you don't have it quite so bad after all.

- Try yoga.
- Appeal to whatever higher power in which you believe.
- Pray.

But most of all…

Get up in the morning. Make your bed. Put on your make-up even if you are working from home. Suit up with your level best (and yes, we mean get dressed every day, even though you may have no place to go) the way you did when you were headed to work. Do this each and every day and treat the day and the world as if all is well or is going to be well.

BECAUSE THAT IS THE WAY IT IS GOING TO BE! Good Luck to all my fellow Baby Boomers.

Toni Kaufman

Toni Kaufman

Toni Kaufman is known for her Radio Show and Podcast, The World Class Mentors, and production/casting background (in English and Spanish) on such famous shows Fremantle Media's Top Talent Searching programs and their Spanish Counterparts... Objetivo Fama, America's Top Models/Belleza Latina and casting families for Family Feud/Que Dice La Gente among many others.

Toni went from owning and managing high-profile corporate teams to creating a network of World Class Mentors that host a multitude of influencers from industries such as oil, technology, speaking, politics and film/TV. These mentors are guests on the show. She is dedicated to celebrating those who have achieved world-class by honoring their mentors, their own lives and legacies. Toni works with entrepreneurs, speakers, authors, healers, and coaches to help them find "The Celebrity Within" she helps her clients fine-tune their message, offers and designs sizzling campaigns to increase sales and bring out their inner hero.

Toni brings a Hi-energy level of empowerment to her audiences, from near-death experiences to driven, absolute entrepreneurship. Motivated-and Inspired are two descriptions of how her audiences leave after her talks.

KDDMWorX programs include Virtually Yours and Online Summit Production Services:

The Game Changer

Our clients redefine their marketing programs and deliver Virtual Assistants and Project Managers that bring the world closer together — we help entrepreneurs, speakers, authors, healers, and coaches delegate their tech work and their social media and online presence. We take your ideas, products or programs, from Concept to Launch and then help them create content for their new TV Channel and distribution network on Entrepreneur's Network.

New 2020 Programs being launched!

Employer/Employee Development Services:
Through our unique offering of ACT2(c) Programs, ACT2 is the right program to help redefine your workforce through self-realization, leadership techniques.

To view Toni's Game Changer Interview, scan the QR code below or follow this link: https://youtu.be/MZGB3_LmAVA

Toni Kaufman

Keep Your Legacy Out of the Graveyard: Live & Leave It!

by Natalie McQueen

Did you ever have something happen in your life that at the time you couldn't believe it was happening to you, but when all was said and done, you look back at that "Game Changer" moment as a blessing in disguise? I did in 2016. It was one of the most terrifying events that I have ever lived through, but the shift in consciousness that I have felt over the past 3 years that is directing me to my soulful, authentic self has been a worthwhile journey.

Life was good. I was in Cuba, celebrating life with Steve, my best friend, and husband of 28 years, and his family. We were exploring and appreciating this unique culture of Cuba. The resort had many restaurants, bars, and areas of relaxation. We spent a day touring Havana and relishing the old buildings, some so beautiful and some almost crumbling to the ground. The next day we made plans to park ourselves at the pool for the day. We enjoyed the sunshine and the swim-up bars with the hospitable Cubans, who loved to make their famous rum drinks. We finally had enough sun and returned to our rooms to shower up and change for dinner. Dinner was delightful as usual. We were told there would be a live local band coming in that night. Having some more drinks and listening to live music sounded like the perfect end to our wonderful day. The band was fabulous. Good times were had by all while tearing it up on the dance floor. After the band ended, Steve and I decided to take a walk on the beach in order to breathe some fresh ocean air.

We walked down the stairs to the beach along the rock wall until we finally arrived at the water's edge. I kicked off my shoes and dipped my toes in the cold water as the waves rolled over my feet and up the front of my legs. I entered the water just up to my knees. At that moment, everything seemed perfect. Caught up in the beautiful surroundings with the moonlight reflecting on the water and the waves crashing on the shoreline, I did not realize that in the next five minutes my world would be turned upside down.

There was a very strong undertow in that area. As I walked a little further, I felt the powerful pull of the water as it engulfed my legs. The next step I took was a big drop and it felt like I was sideswiped when both of my legs were pulled out from underneath me. My body became fully submerged in the water and I felt a panic rush through my body as I was being taken out to sea. My husband frantically reached out for me; he tried to grab me, but the force of the waves was too strong for me to hang on. I was pulled down under the swirling current, under the edge of the rock wall, and no longer in Steve's sight.

My body was being smashed and thrown around by the waves. I don't really remember all that occurred since everything suddenly went black. I was not sure which direction was up to the surface, but I knew I had to get some air very soon. Pressure started building up in my lungs and I wanted to breathe, but I knew that was not a choice at the moment. When I finally surfaced, I realized the beautiful moonlight that was above me earlier was not there anymore. It was replaced by a jagged black rock wall over my head. I gasped for breath, trying to stabilize myself. As soon as I was able to fill my lungs with air, another huge wave hit me from behind and then dragged me back out to sea.

I felt so helpless; the water's power was so strong, tossing me all over the place from one side to the other like a rag doll. Then, the other current pushed me forcefully against the rock wall. I used my arms and shins to protect my head as they hit the wall first. I felt the sting of the sharp rock edges cutting into my skin. I was stuck between these two different currents of water. One pulled me down under the water while I held my breath and hoped I had enough air until I was hit by the other force of water that would crush me into the rock wall once again. This back and forth movement made me feel very disoriented and I could hear my heart pounding inside of my ears.

I knew I had to get out from between these two currents. I had been a fairly confident swimmer, so I was never afraid of drowning, but at that moment, I felt like there wasn't going to be a way out of that place! I held my breath as long as I could. Time went by very slowly, especially when I was dragged deep under the water, not knowing when my next breath would be. It seemed like everything was in slow motion. It was so dark, but I knew that once again I would have to brace myself for the impact using my shins and arms to protect myself against a fatal head injury. My body was beginning to feel so exhausted; I realized I wasn't going to be able to withstand this energy-draining situation much longer.

The waves were getting stronger and faster. It became harder and harder to get a full breath before the next wave arrived. Now it seemed like I could only gasp in a partial breath before I was pulled back under. It was like I was trapped in a nightmare and I was waiting to wake up at any moment. It was very hard to think logically. I was not able to formulate a strategy in my mind in order to take control of the situation and save myself. I had no concept of how much time had passed. I didn't even know whether there was a way to get out, but I knew I needed to try.

My body was so tired from being tossed around and fighting for the next bit of oxygen that I could get into my lungs. I do remember being grateful when I was able to fill my lungs with a full breath before going back under. It felt like a little bit of peace came over my body. I realized I could not hear the crashing of the waves anymore. It felt like I was in a dark tunnel filled with a silent buzzing of white noise. Oddly enough, I was not frightened at that point; I could only feel peace and calm. I was getting used to the rhythm of the waves pulling me out toward the deeper sea and then crashing into the wall. I knew when to brace myself and when to fill my lungs for the next plunge.

Despite being depleted of energy, I recall thinking I needed to keep on fighting, but my muscles were no longer responding. Even the idea of taking in a breath of water knowing it would end this fight crossed my mind. When I really started contemplating what that would mean and how it would affect the people in my life… suddenly, it felt like someone slapped me on the back of my head to get my attention. Flashbacks of memories of all the people in my life that I love were coming to my mind. It was like they were right in front of me, instead of just inside my head. I could see their future without me. My loving husband would be a widower, raising our two beautiful daughters alone. My parents, my brother, my in-laws, and my two sisters-in-law would have to plan my funeral.

There are so many things I have not yet said, romantic trips I have not

not yet taken, mother/daughter and fun family times that still need to happen. I couldn't imagine how my daughters would grow up without a mother; how alone and sad they would feel. I want to see their graduations and weddings, enjoy the grand-dogs, grand-bunnies, grand-birds and someday, grandchildren. I did not want to miss out on their entire lives. My husband and I have so many amazing bucket list items to still scratch off together. I want to tell all the amazing people in my life how much I love them and how much they mean to me. I want to live out my bucket list and enjoy life to the fullest!

I had to make a decision about whether I wanted to let my exhausted body win or fight to get back home with my family. I decided I was going to do everything in my power to save myself. I wasn't ready to leave my life behind and I was not going to allow myself any other option. This was truly my "Game Changer Moment!

After I made up my mind, I heard voices not too far away from me. I could see off to the right the moonlight reflecting off the water again. The waves were still throwing my tired body around, but I put every drop of my energy into shifting my body to go toward the moonlight. I finally came out from under the cliff's edge and saw an even brighter light coming from the sky. For the first time in what felt like a lifetime of struggling to survive, I felt hope that I was going to get out alive. I did not know the source of the light, but I swam toward it and the waters seemed to calm down.

I was now in an alcove where I could touch the bottom with my feet and was able to stand and let myself finally start to relax. I heard people shouting my name and I recognized the voices of my family. A rescue team dropped a very long ladder down the side of the cliff to get me. It became clear to me that the bright light was the rescue team's spotlight. Before I knew it, I was being helped up the ladder by one of the rescuers.

I was guided up the ladder to the top of the cliff, where I was reunited with my husband, sister-in-law, and my mother and father-in-law. They were extremely traumatized and shocked; they had been crying and praying for a good outcome the whole time I was in the water. They hugged me and I really felt their love and presence.

The Game Changer

I was trying to take in what had just happened to me. The rescuing team could not believe that I was alive. They informed me that the undertow was so strong that there was barely any chance of survival. They explained to my husband and his parents that if I were to have drowned, they wouldn't have been able to find my body. I felt incredibly sad that I had caused them such a worrisome and traumatic experience up top, while I was experiencing my own down below. I did not know how long I was in the water fighting for my life, but I later learned that I was down under the cliff for more than an hour.

After reflecting and feeling such gratitude for being alive, I realized that I had to change my life and live with continual gratitude in my heart, nurturing relationships to the fullest, sharing life's lessons with those I love, making sure the important people in my life know that they are loved. It was not my time to go – I have too much to do and experience with the people that mean the most to me! It really had me thinking, "what would I have wanted to leave behind for my husband, daughters, parents, and family? Did they know how much I loved them? What wisdom could I have imparted to them? What mistakes had I made in my life that if they knew, maybe they wouldn't have to repeat?" I would want to share with them my funny stories from childhood that perhaps they didn't know. I would like to share with them what matters the most in my life and why, as well as what my years of life experience taught me to do and not to do.

Once a person goes through a life-changing event like this, it is impossible to go back to who you were before. I felt something change in me. It was like my heart was about to explode with appreciation for getting another chance. Although I would never want to go through such a traumatic experience again, it has changed my perspective on how I live life. I try not to negatively dwell on what happened to me.

Instead, I choose to see it as a wake-up call to start living the life I was meant to live. Having that near-death experience has made me analyze my previous actions. Most of my choices were for acceptance, to please someone, to not rock the boat. Often, I would not share my true feelings because I did not want to hurt someone's feelings, so I would push down my true voice and just smile. I now understand that constraining my true feelings impacted me and my other relationships very negatively.

I have reflected in gratitude on my relationships that I have in my life. I am so blessed to have so many amazing people that make my world a better place. I have also realized that I have some relationships in my life that are not positive and take up too much of my time. Knowing that time is precious and what we do with it is ultimately our decision, I now focus on growing those relationships that enhance my life and make me a better person. I am responsible for my life so why not make it amazing with people that want to do the same! We all see the world differently because of our life experiences and we have stories to share that could impact others. We are all on a journey do not know when our journey will end, so we must make the most of it.

Legacy is one of the most important things that you can create and leave to carry on your life lessons to make an impact on other people's lives. Who is a better person because of you? Do you make the people around you laugh and smile? We all have stories and wisdom to share that may not seem extraordinary or life-changing to you, but if you passed away without sharing these experiences - the world would be missing out. You never know the impact that one of your stories could make on one person, that in turn, takes your story and creates a ripple effect, touching many lives.

A recent experience of mine is a perfect example of a life-touching story. My grandmother was turning 100 years old and our family created a legacy book for her, using her own words and stories for the first couple of chapters. Then each family member wrote their own chapter. Although I knew how amazing my grandmother was, I had no idea that creating and sharing her life story would have such an incredible effect on my life, as well as all those that loved her.

As a partner in a publishing company, the biggest challenge we hear is how to get started and that is where we can help you. Don't let fear hold you back from sharing your story, your wisdom, and your impact on the world! Do not wait any longer to start to leave your legacy for future generations to enjoy and pass on. In this day and age of technology, it is easier than ever to share your legacy!

Wouldn't it feel good to know that if something were to happen to you, you had prepared by having everything you wanted to share with your loved ones, everything that you wanted to say to the people you are left behind, a reflection of your true heart, values, and memories all put together in a beautiful legacy book that your loved ones will have forever?

"The graveyard is the richest place on earth, because it is here that you will find all the hopes and dreams that were never fulfilled, the books that were never written, the songs that were never sung, the inventions that were never shared, the cures that were never discovered, all because someone was too afraid to take the first step, keep with the problem, or determine to carry out their dream." - Les Brown

To view Natalie's Game Changer video interview, scan the QR Code below or follow this link: https://youtu.be/qebhJEm3fb0

Natalie McQueen

Natalie McQueen

Natalie McQueen is the Director of Marketing and Sales at Spotlight Publishing. Natalie has a background in finance, sales, marketing, and has trained with mindset development for many years.

She coaches Entrepreneurs to Unleash their Authority and Expertise through Authorship implementing the right combination of marketing strategies, tools, and techniques that will keep their bookselling long after their publishing date has passed.

The Spotlight Publishing team has brought over 220 authors to #1 Bestseller due to a unique and powerful marketing system.

When Natalie is not dreaming big with authors, she enjoys dates nights with her husband Steve of 28 years! They love to travel together and spend time as a family. Their two daughters, Taylor & Kayla keep them thinking young, and playing hard especially at Dave Matthew's Concerts!

Website - https://spotlightpublishing.pro/
LinkedIn - https://www.linkedin.com/in/nataliemcqueen/
Twitter - https://twitter.com/NatalieQueen22
Facebook - https://www.facebook.com/NatalieMcQueen22
Facebook Business Page -
https://www.facebook.com/Spotlightonyourbusiness/

Best Day / Worst Day

by Melodee Meyer

Sometimes the best day can be the worst day.

I was sitting at my computer, refreshing the UPS website every two minutes trying to see if there was an update on my package. It still read, "Out for delivery" when suddenly I heard footsteps at the front door. It was here!

I had been waiting for years for this day and it had finally arrived.

The delivery guy seemed to be moving in slow motion so I impatiently stepped forward to take the box out of his arms. I almost dropped it. The box was much heavier than I thought.

"Your name," he asked.

"Meyer," I said proudly and pointed to the name on the box now sitting on the floor.

"Okay, have a good day."

"Oh, I am having the best day," I said to him as he walked out.

Ah, finally. Let's do this.

I looked for scissors. *How come I can never find scissors when I need them?* I grabbed a pen and just started stabbing at the tape holding the box seam together. I worked my fingers into the holes the pen had made and tore open the top of the box. I lifted the brown packing paper… and there it was. My book.

I was a published author and here was my first box of books, delivered to my doorstep. I squealed.

I pulled one out. It had that "new car" smell. The cover felt like suede. I flipped through it. Wow. This was all really happening.

It had taken years to get to this day. I had always wanted to be an author. It had been on my dream board for at least ten years. I even wrote an article for my elementary school newspaper when I was nine and announced I would write a book someday. And now someday was today.

Although I had a lot of experience writing, I had zero experience with publishing so once I had written my book I started looking for a publisher. I had no idea it would be so difficult. Apparently traditional publishers only want to publish books by well-known authors and celebrities — and I was neither.

Publishing was a huge mystery to me. And the more I looked into it, the more mysterious it seemed. After much investigation, I settled on a publisher I heard about through a friend that fell into the category of a "hybrid publisher". Hybrid publishing is a special gray area between traditional publishing and self-publishing. It sounded appealing to me, after all, I did not want to self publish. I had seen books that were self-published and they did not have the professional look I wanted.

This hybrid publisher said they would take care of everything: editing, cover design, interior layout, ISBN numbers, publishing, distribution, printing and a bunch of other stuff that I didn't even know I needed. Phew! Was I glad to find them! And all they wanted in return was money.

Who says you can't throw money at a problem and make it go away? *Look! I have a real book!*

I took pictures, I streamed live on social media, I called my mom. This was a best the day, ever!

Once my heart stopped racing, I sat down to read it. Yes, I had written it but now I wanted to read it as a *book*.

But something was wrong… very, very wrong.

The Game Changer

Wait a second, what's this? There was a misprinted page, right at the beginning of the book. My heart stopped. I started flipping through the book. *Oh no!* The publisher had printed the wrong manuscript. They had printed an earlier draft of the book that hadn't been corrected.

I grabbed another book out of the box. I flipped through it desperately. *The same.* I had an entire box of books printed from the wrong manuscript! It was then that I realized that this was not the worst of it.

My book was a #1 bestseller and almost 2,000 books were sent out from the first printing. That meant that everybody got the wrong book. This was no longer the best day.

The publisher's response? "Oh, sorry but it was really your fault because you rushed us." *What?* They said that if I sent them back the books, they would replace them. I couldn't send back thousands of books that had already been delivered around the world!

Well, when life gives you lemons, grab the tequila and salt – and then get back to work. I had more books to write but needless to say, I had to figure out this publishing piece. There was no way I was going to delegate something this important to anyone again without first understanding it myself.

This was a defining moment. I was going to take responsibility for this, even if the publisher was not. You see, I knew what it was to be a victim. But those days were long over.

I had been the target of bullying when I was in seventh grade. Apparently, the kids at my school didn't like other kids who got good grades and who were highlighted by the teacher. They didn't like it one bit.

It started with me getting shoved into lockers and tripped in the hallway. It turned into stealing my lunch, then my homework and my schoolbooks. From there it escalated to getting punched and kicked and laughed at. I don't know what hurt more, the physical abuse or the absolute loneliness and isolation that I felt.

My parents had no idea what was going on. All they knew is that their star student was about to fail her classes. Fortunately, they decided to buy a new house on the other side of town so I was able to start anew and leave that victim persona behind. Or so I thought.

After high school, I married the first guy who said he loved me. He did his best but unbeknownst to either of us, he was dealing with a bipolar disorder that sent him into rages and sent me to the hospital and hiding in a women's shelter with my kids.

The road to my recovery was long and challenging. I had to learn how to love myself and how to set boundaries. What I discovered was that I was resilient and resourceful and powerful. I was not a victim. I was the author of my own life.

So I was not about to let this publishing setback define me. I had paid this company about $20,000 that I was never going to see again. *Get over it. Education is expensive.* I was going to learn what I needed to learn to move up and move on.

What I learned was shocking. Self-publishing had changed drastically in the last five years and was very simple to do. I learned that self-published books didn't have to look homemade and they could still be sold in bookstores and they could still be picked up by agents and big house publishers. *Who knew?*

After I self-published my next book and made it a bestseller, one of my friends asked me to help them with theirs. Then a client asked me to help them too and before I knew it, I was coaching a bunch of people and walking them step-by-step through the process of writing and publishing their own books.

If that publisher had not made the mistake they made, I would not have learned what I did and I would not have the relationships and connections that I have enjoyed for the last several years.

What I learned is that if you read a story and it has an unhappy ending, the story isn't finished yet. You just have to read a little further because eventually, it gets happy again. Sometimes the best day can be the worst day and yet can also be the best day.

Melodee Meyer

Melodee Meyer is a 6th-degree black belt, an international bestselling author, keynote speaker and business advisor to entrepreneurs and passionate leaders who want to make a positive impact in the world. Melodee teaches her clients how to get on TV and is the host of The Mission-Driven Entrepreneur Show. She is the creator of the Ultimate Bestseller Formula, an online program designed to help coaches, consultants, and other experts become a bestselling author in 60 days or less.

www.MelodeeMeyer.com

To view Melodee's interview for The Game Changer, scan the QR Code below or follow this link: https://youtu.be/V_bbVP3oL0k

Melodee Meyer

About Iman Aghay

Iman Aghay

Iman Aghay is a serial entrepreneur, best-selling author, and international speaker. He founded *Success Road Academy* in 2010, which is one of the largest Information Marketing Training Centers in the world. He harnesses the power of the Internet and combines it with effective in-person marketing to help business owners grow their companies, and professionals position themselves as the go-to experts in their fields.

Also, he is the creator of *"Ultimate Course Formula,"* which helps experts create and sell online courses with a simple step by step process in 60 days or less.

Iman has worked with over 15,000 business owners in the past few years in his seminars, events, webinars, group coaching, and one on one coaching sessions.

Iman is a TEDx speaker and has spoken on the stage over 400 times in

the past few years, in front of audiences of thousands of people. He has the stage with Gary Vaynerchuk, Dan Martell, Sean Stephenson, Ted McGrath, John Chow as well as presenters from the David Suzuki

Iman Aghay

Foundation, Hootsuite, Yelp and many others.

Iman arrived in Vancouver in 2009 with limited knowledge of English, no network, and no job. After studying the most successful businesses in the world, he created a marketing system that combined the most effective marketing strategies used by those businesses. He started his own company, applied his system and in a very short time:

- Founded Entrepreneurs International Network, which is a group of business networks in 5 countries in the world with over 20,000 members today.
- Founded the largest information marketing training center in Canada, *"Success Road Academy"* with over 10,000 attendees to its events in the past three years.
- Taught his system and helped thousands of people to build successful businesses for themselves. Today he has clients from Courtney, Canada to Sidney, Australia.

He has been featured on CBC radio, Shaw TV, Fox, CBS News, ABC, NBC and has made the cover of Immigrants Magazine. Iman's passion is helping entrepreneurs to succeed. He won the People's Choice Award for being one of the top 25 immigrants in Canada and shares this honor with media mogul Peter Legge, Dragon's Den star Robert Herjavec and John Furlong, CEO of Vancouver Organizing Committee for the 2010 Olympic and Paralympic Winter Games.

View Iman's Game Changer video interview by scanning the QR Code below or clicking on this link: https://youtu.be/vLIW_DTal6Q

Made in the USA
Columbia, SC
23 December 2019